WHAT IS LANDSCAPE?

MICHAEL JAKOB

INDEX

I	The Omni-Landscape	4
II	"A landscape is a landscape is a landscape…"	16
III	For a Definition of Landscape	28
IV	Landscape and Time	50
V	From the Picturesque to the Postmodern	98
VI	Problems and future Perspectives	138

CHAPTER I

THE OMNI-LANDSCAPE

INTRODUCTION

Our age is clearly the age of landscape, at least as far as its verbal reproduction and its iconic representation are concerned. Both the word and the phenomenon are there for all to witness, in daily press and specialized journals, on screens and walls, via representations or in the consciousness of the beholder. Nowadays landscape is shown off and unveiled, discussed and flattered, preserved and protected, and equally sold and resold. Popularized and democratized, landscape now belongs to everyone, while, in the past, it played the role of a social code and was the hallmark of an elite, which willingly identified itself with the common sharing of symbolic places or topical representations.

The contemporary debate on landscape is no longer expressed through the exclusive idiolect of a social class. We are instead confronted with a relentless landscape chatter, which invades every domain of daily life. Human sciences have participated in this tendency as well, feeding the landscape-discourse with an impressive amount of articles, collective works and debates on the subject. Once marginal, landscape has become central, if not essential to aesthetics and geography[1], while strengthening its position within sociological, anthropological and archaeological theories[2].

The new status of landscape represents an international phenomenon that transcends traditional linguistic and disciplinary boundaries. Thanks to the universal circulation of images in the media, even societies that did not possess the terms to designate

---

1. C. Raffestin, *Du paysage à l'espace ou les signes de la géographie,* in «Hérodote», 1978, 9, 90-104; A. Bailly, C. Raffestin, H. Reymond, *Les concepts du paysage: problématique et représentations*, in «L'Espace géographique», 1980, IX, 4, 277-286; Y. Lacoste, *A quoi sert le paysage? Qu'est-ce qu'un beau paysage?,* in *La théorie du paysage en France 1794-1994,* ed. A. Roger, Champ Vallon, Seyssel 1995, 42-73.

2. See the works of Marc Augé, increasingly focused on landscape (*Nonlieux, introduction à une anthropologie de la surmodernité*, Le Seuil, Paris 1992; transl.: *Non-Places: An Introduction to Supermodernity,* Verso, London 2008; *L'impossible voyage. Le tourisme et ses images,* Payot & Rivages, Paris 1997; *Le temps en ruines,* Galilée, Paris 2003.) For archaeology and landscape: C. Tilley, *A Phenomenology of Landscape. Places, Paths and Monuments,* Berg, Oxford 1994; G. Rapp, C.L. Hill, *Geoarchaeology: The Earth Science Approach to Archaeological Interpretation*, Yale University Press, New Haven 1998; J. Rossignol, L.A. Wandsnider, *Space, Time, and Archaeological Landscapes,* Plenum Press, New York 1992.

landscape can now easily identify and get to know it. Landscape is therefore not only the characteristic expression of a globalised world; it is also one of the essential aspects that contributes to the increasing uniformity of visual schemes, concepts, and design solutions. Facing the success of the by-now ubiquitous landscape, we must nevertheless ask ourselves: what have we lost by living in the age of landscape? Does not the hypertrophy of landscape, namely its extreme visibility and its fashionable status, hide something else? What is the actual cost of landscape and what of its forgotten—or, rather, repressed—counterpart, the land? Every kind of cultural overexposure refers to a concealed polar opposite and to an absent signifier. It is therefore crucial to analyze the mental and psychic representations of landscape and raise some fundamental questions, such as: what do we mean today by using the term "landscape"? Confronted with the general context of landscape's current glory we have to ask ourselves, for which reasons this specific phenomenon has attained universality. The dynamism of the debate on contemporary landscape theory points to a complex phenomenon. Landscape's reality comes from far away and has a hidden history, an ideology, a point of view that became dominant over time. Whether landscape is a *Eurocentric* reality disguised as a universal one, or, on the contrary, an anthropological feature developed for accidental reasons in Europe, is still the matter of discussion. The reasons for the present success of landscape could—at first sight—refer to the rise of the environmental movement. Modern ecology is, however, not the indispensable condition of the *omni-landscape*. Both environmental and landscape awareness, as well as the fascination with nature and the fascination with landscape, are part of a larger trend related to the relationship of the post-modern individual with nature.

Throughout history, it has always been the city that invented and defined its counterpart—landscape—by preaching the "return to nature". The dominant city has created its "outside", that is, the "countryside", the "peripheral", the "regional", the "exotic", and it has generated as well the national parks, the concept of natural heritage and, of course, landscape itself. The increasing distance from nature has always caused the desire to go back to it.

From this point of view, the environmental movement of the 1970s represents a reiteration[3], since it was, once again, the discomfort in the city and the urban crisis that caused the demand for more nature. The contemporary *omni-city*—the absolute supremacy of the city—has attracted mankind into the urban realm while at the same time pushing people outside, towards more or less preserved natural *enclaves*[4].

The contemporary hunger for landscape represents—from this point of view—the recurrence of a historical phenomenon, connected to the dialectic of the urban versus the rural, the city versus nature[5]. The current situation repeats and varies a state of affairs, which the Hellenistic culture of the third century B.C. already knew very well; so did Augustan and Renaissance Italy[6]. However, two new aspects characterize the decades of the late twentieth-century, marked by the flourishing interest in nature. The first one regards the post-war planning crisis and the increasing dissolution of the usual distinctions between the main poles of the territorial system: city-country-side(primeval) nature. Earlier on, it had always been possible to identify and discern between the different entities existing in a territory and to separate them both conceptually and administratively[7]. The phenomenon of sprawl[8], the urbanization of small towns and sport resorts, the crisis of agriculture[9] and of traditional industrial

3. See L. Trepl, *Geschichte der Ökologie: vom 17. Jahrhundert bis zur Gegenwart*, Athenäum Frankfurt am Main 1987. For ancient ecology: P. Fedeli, *La natura violata. Ecologia e mondo romano*, Sellerio, Palermo 1990. For the «malaise» of those years see especially: I. McHarg, *Design with Nature*, Wiley New York 1992.
4. See I. Calvino, *Marcovaldo ovvero le stagioni in città*, Einaudi, Turin 1966 (transl.: *Marcovaldo or the Seasons in the City*, Vintage, London 2001).
5. See F. Sengle, *Wunschbild Land und Schreckensbild Stadt: zu einem zentralen Thema der neueren deutschen Literatur*, in «Studium Generale», 1963, XVI, vol. 10, 619-631; J. Dixon Hunt, *L'art du jardin et son histoire*, Odile Jacob, Paris 1996; G. Böhme, *Für eine ökologische Naturästhetik*, Suhrkamp, Frankfurt am Main 1999.
6. See N. Elias, Über den Prozess der Zivilisation, Haus zum Falken, Basel 1939 (transl.: *The Civilizing Process. Sociogenetic and Psychogenetic Investigations*, Blackwell, Oxford 1982).
7. It's still the case in the three famous programmatic articles of J. C. Rose, D. Kiley and G. Eckbo: *Landscape Design in the Primeval Environment*, in «Architectural Record», February 1940, 74-79; *Landscape Design in the Rural Environment*, in «Architectural Record», August 1939; *Landscape Design in the Urban Environment*, in «Architectural Record», May 1939, 70-76.
8. See R. Ingersoll, *Sprawltown: Looking for the City on Its Edges*, Princeton Architectural Press, New York 2006; A. Berger, *Drosscape: Wasting Land in Urban America*, Princeton Architectural Press, New York 2007.
9. See G. Duby, A. Wallon, *Histoire de la France rurale*. vol. III, *Apogée et crise de la civilisation paysanne (1789-1914)*, Gallimard, Paris 1975.

activities, followed by the exponential rise of urban fringes, all of this transformed well-known territories into an increasingly illegible reality. The lack of references and the daily exposure to faceless "non-places" and interstitial zones[10] have motivated the yearning to identify, protect, and celebrate identifiable territories, well defined places of leisure, wild landscapes, or picturesque sites. Hence the paradoxical aspiration—within a territorial fabric in continuous evolution—to determine the exact sense of precise places, to celebrate the identity of landscape, to map (for example thanks to strategies of *visual assessment*[11], to exhibit[12]), or to delineate landscapes by inscribing their specificity in equivocal texts of the sort of the "Great Book" of World Heritage sites.

UNESCO's project has undoubtedly contributed to making landscape more popular. Heritage sites that need to be preserved at all cost have aroused public awareness and stimulated those eager to include "their" favorite landscapes into the World Heritage list. UNESCO's catalogue had—directly and indirectly—political, economic, and social repercussions and it gave rise to politics of image based representations on a large scale. This operation appears, at first glance, to be the answer to the citizens' natural need for nature in a world characterized by increased territorial mutability. However the idea of establishing a universal heritage catalogue has however a troublesome and ambiguous origin. It is the result of the Aswan dam scheme, that is the modernization of Egypt and its main side-effect, the relocation of Abu Simbel[13] (Ill. 1). It was literally the loss and the wound, the wide ranging alteration of an area of prime archeological interest that caused the technologic and semiotic operation culminating with the recreation of Abu Simbel. The consequence

---

10. See M. Augé, *Non-lieux*, 97- 144; T. Sieverts, *Zwischenstadt, zwischen Ort und Welt, Raum und Zeit, Stadt und Land*, Vieweg, Braunschweig-Wiesbaden 1999 (transl.: *Cities without Cities: An interpretation of the Zwischenstadt*, Routledge, London/ New York: 2003.
11. See *Guidelines for Landscape and Visual Impact Assessment*, The Landscape Institute, London 2002.
12. See *Paysages photographies: la mission photographique de la DATAR, travaux en cours 1984-1985*, Hazan, Paris 1985; *Paysages photographies: en France les années quatre-vingt: 1984-1988, la mission photographique de la DATAR*, Hazan, Paris 1989.
13. The operation of Abu Simbel has been financed with US funds (CIA); it represents a manipulation of the Egyptian site both on a political and a territorial level.

1 The Relocation of Abu Simbel, Egypt, 1964-1972

of a relocated and previously dismantled reality and the result of a territorial crisis (in the etymological sense of the Greek word *krisis*: "cut", "separation"), Abu Simbel is the symbol of a generalized practice in the field of "heritage": the majority of protected sites and landscapes worldwide are, actually, constructions, collages, patchwork. Our well-guarded "good" landscapes are palimpsests identified as "natural" only because they are registered in a comprehensive catalogue.

The second aspect to keep in mind is the contemporary status of the image and its impact on landscape. A famous photograph from June 1969 (*The Blue Marble*, Ill. 2) shows our planet as seen from the moon. It confronts us—from a distance and thanks to the mediation of technology—with the planet we inhabit and, simultaneously, provides an unusual view and a new epistemological framework. While the beauty and vulnerability of Earth appealed to the aesthetic sense, the surprising appearance of the Earth seen as a whole—never before had our planet been empirically perceivable in this way—allowed the development of the concept of biosphere[14]. It was partly *Blue Marble*, a picture beyond landscape photography, that fostered the ecological debate and redefined the way of interpreting and managing nature. Other *clichés*, for instance that of the lunar landscape with the American flag (Ill. 3), endlessly repeated on TV screens and in the printed press, had a considerable impact as well. In the contemporary ultra-technological society everything seems to exist only to become a powerful image.

Today, landscape is at the center of a sophisticated semiotic network. There are, on the one hand and on a planetary scale, billions of landscape-photographs that haunt us from screens, billboards or newspapers. On the other hand, there exist billions of landscape-photographs that we create while travelling, our landscape-albums and landscape-sequences. Nowadays the world's tourism industry and the digital image industry have, nowadays, a direct effect on our way of discovering and memorizing reality. The circulation of images

---

14. In September 1970, the magazine «Scientific American» published a special issue entitled *The Biosphere*. The introduction reads "Photographs of the earth show that it has a green-blue color. [...] The biosphere—this thin film of air and water and soil and life no deeper than ten miles, or the one four-hundredth of the earth's radius—is now the setting of the uncertain history of man."

2 *The Blue Marble*, Apollo 17, december 7, 1972

is the most efficient and the most ambiguous expression of the omni-landscape. The fact that our travels are motivated by the amount of landscape-photographs we can bring home and that the points of view we use in order to frame the most "beautiful" landscapes is so often predefined pose serious threats to our spontaneity. Landscape-photographs even penetrate our dreams, and they also influence the way in which we inhabit the world. Many gated communities reproduce standardized landscape types, the picturesque code of the postcard landscape, and touristic resorts around the world do the same, they present 'superior' landscapes that correspond to a homogenized model.

These recent developments concern, of course, the authenticity of the experience of landscape. Contemporary landscapes appear—in light of the above—to be directed or manipulated by a powerful discourse on landscape and its predefined models. Hence, landscape turns out to be the standardized product of a consumer society. Whilst feeling free to enjoy the most diverse landscapes, we actually are subjected to the conditioning of a cultural and economic process. The reality of landscape turns out to be, using a Heideggerian terminology, *uneigentlich*, fundamentally inauthentic. When experiencing landscape, we expose ourselves to the arbitrariness (*Willkürlichkeit*) and to the randomness (*Beliebigkeit*) of a practice dominated by the anonymous perspective of a collective point of view[15].

The frenetic circulation of image based landscapes in the mind of people and the contemporary touristic practice appear to support such hypotheses. The landscape as a commonplace par excellence (landscapes of escape, postcard-landscapes, dreamscapes, exotic landscapes, etc.) seems to correspond perfectly to the idea of an average aesthetic value (*Durchschnittlichkeit*)[16], imposed by force by others without our knowledge.

Criticizing the inauthenticity of today's landscape implies, however, the existence of a point of view able to define an authentic landscape. A landscape could be considered to be authentic if given, to someone, by surprise, and not when given to everyone in a general sense; it would appear as authentic when someone *discovers* a piece

---

15. M. Heidegger, *Sein und Zeit*, Max Niemeyer, Tübingen 1963, § 27 (transl.: *Being and Time*, State University of New York Press, Albany/ New York 1996.
16. *Ibid.*, 127.

3 Apollo 11 astronaut Edwin «Buzz» Aldrin Jr. salutes the U.S. flag, July 20, 1969

of nature, and not when the same person simply re-cognizes a piece of nature on the basis of a pre-existent model. Such landscape, if we were to admit its existence, would break with daily life and its patterns, instead of reproducing them in a more or less ritualized manner. Authentic landscape would imply a free subject and not a representative of a society guided by opaque schemes. Such a landscape would momentarily unite the subject in question with the totality of nature—as superbly expressed by Goethe in "*The Sorrows of Young Werther*"[17]— instead of leaving her or him in front of a distant nature that remains forever outside, that is before the eyes of its beholder. It would also imply the synesthetic presence of all senses, instead of a passive submission to the command of the eye and to the semantics of vision.

As an exception and as an event, authentic landscape frees itself from the dictatorship of the standardized modes of the scopic interpretation of the world. Authentic landscape, however, does not last long. It disappears immediately, once the 'normal' perspective of everyday life is regained, and turns into an indescribable phenomenon. We can communicate and share the essence of 'normal' events, but landscape—as an interruption and interval—can hardly be mediated. (We can say that we *had* this experience, but we cannot describe it properly.) Yet authentic landscape should by no means be understood as the opposite of or the remedy to the omni-landscape. As an extreme—an antithesis to the extreme of the stereotype-landscapes—, it represents rather an ideal indebted to Kantian philosophy (and the supposed purity of aesthetic experience) and to the world view of the post-Romantic hero, a fundamentally solitary subject, who perceives his whole life through the lens of his encounter with nature.

Authentic landscape and its opposite, non-authentic landscape, do not exist. Landscape has always progressed as a mediation between two poles, individual and collective, active and passive, free and guided. The radical stance of the "authentic" model has, however, a major role: it reminds us that, with the experience of landscape, it is the essence of the self that is at stake.

17. See J. W. Goethe, *The Sorrows of Young Werther*, Penguin, London 1989, May 10th letter.

CHAPTER II

"A LANDSCAPE
IS A LANDSCAPE
IS A LANDSCAPE…"

The discourse on landscape—in the Foucauldian meaning of the word «discourse»—represents the totality of the elements which directly or indirectly influence landscape. Influence is here preferred to regulation or imposition, given the complexity of the multifaceted relations at stake. The concept of discourse pertains to linguistics, rhetoric, and hermeneutics[1]. The exaggerated visibility underlying the concept of "omni-landscape" does not only refer to an excessive debate on landscape (architects, urban planners, landscape architects, artists, light designers, politicians, the press—everyone is discussing landscape these days), it consists of the very fact of talking about it. Landscape, primarily a non-verbal phenomenon, therefore gets inscribed in a verbal flux, a discourse.

The discourse on landscape, by definition, manifests itself in various ways. Landscape is called and written in thousands of manners, thousands of different contexts. One of the cornerstones of the present debate is represented by the so called theories of landscape. The theories of the last decades are nothing but a huge intertext. Alain Roger supplies a perfect demonstration of this fact with his key concept of *artialisation*, according to which a "land" does not become a "landscape" unless "under the domination of art"[2]. The theory of *artialisation* draws its central argument from Charles Lalo[3], who resumes it from Montaigne. The opposition between land and landscape recalls furthermore an often cited quotation from the essay *De la composition des paysages* by the Marquis de Girardin: "Along the great paths, and also in the paintings of mediocre artists, one sees nothing but the *land*. But a landscape, a poetic scene, is a situation chosen or *created* through tastes and feelings"[4]. Or, in Alain Roger's words: "Nature is indeterminate and only receives its determination through art: the land becomes landscape only under the influence of a Landscape,

1. See M. Foucault, *Réponse à une question*, in «Esprit», May 1968, 5, 6, 851-874; *L'archéologie du savoir*, Gallimard, Paris 1969 (transl.: *The archaeology of knowledge*, Routledge, London 1999; *L'ordre du discours*, Gallimard, Paris 1971; M. Frank, *Zum Diskurs-Begriff bei Foucault*, in *Diskurstheorien und Literaturwissenschaft*, ed. J. Fohrmann and H. Müller, Suhrkamp, Frankfurt am Main 1989, 25-44.

2. A. Roger, *Histoire d'une passion théorique ou comment on devient un Raboliot du paysage*, in *La théorie du paysage en France 1794-1994*, ed. A. Roger, Champ Vallon, Seyssel 1995, 438-451 and 441 ss.; Id. *Court traité du paysage*, Gallimard, Paris 1997, 11 ss.

3. See Ch. Lalo, *Introduction à l'esthétique*, Colin, Paris 1912.

4. René-Louis de Girardin, De la composition du paysage, Delaguette, Geneva 1777, 64.

and this happens according to the two methods of *artialisation*, the direct or the indirect interaction"[5]. Later on, Roger makes reference to Rabelais's *Gargantua and Pantagruel* (ch. XVI) and to the writer Henri Cueco, from whom he quotes the following passage:

> *Louis, how do you say: is the landscape beautiful?* He looks at me and I understand I'm posing a difficult question. After a long silence he finally answers: *es brave lo païs, on dit.* I see, there is no word for *landscape* in Occitan. [...] The initial misunderstanding wasn't only due to the usual linguistic difficulties, but also to the misunderstanding of the very concept of landscape. Landscape, to him and his people, is the country[6].

In his "theory", Roger resorts to anecdotes (for instance, Cézanne's often cited legend of the farmer who "had never seen Sainte-Victoire"[7], neologisms (he speaks of écolonisation, a combination between "ecology" and "colonization", of *géophagie*[8], Geophagia), and witty wordplays (the landscape, *paysage,* is the *pays sage*[9], the diligent land). The scientific ambition—the author claims to finally deliver a "doctrine of landscape", "a legitimate theoretical and systematic treatise on the matter"[10]—is based on the proliferation of figures of speech and second hand occurrences, which transform the founding text into a large collage or an endlessly readjusted assemblage.

The need—especially in French or German "theory"—to resort to personifications such as: the "death" of landscape[11], the "birth" of landscape, or the "invention" of landscape, emphasizes in particular the strategies of the staging of the object to be defined, presented in a seemingly objective manner. The second introduction that Denis Cosgrove published on the occasion of the publication of *Social Formation and Symbolic Landscape* in 1998 shows—within a completely different socio-cultural context marked by a far more pragmatic approach—a similar penchant for a discursive, that is text-oriented approach of

---

5. A. Roger, *Court traité du paysage*, 443.
6. A. Roger, *Histoire d'une passion théorique*, 444; Id., *Court traité du paysage*, 24-25.
7. A. Roger, *Histoire d'une passion théorique*, 445; Id., *Court traité du paysage*, 21.
8. Roger, *Histoire d'une passion théorique*, 449.
9. *Ibid.*, 446. [The wordplay is based on the word *sage* which, in French, means *wise*].
10. Roger, *Court traité du paysage*, 7.
11. F. Dagognet, *Mort du paysage? Philosophie et esthétique du paysage*, Champ Vallon, Seyssel 1982.

landscape[12]. In his critical (auto-)reinterpretation, the British geographer wishes—from the start—to point out his debt towards two eminent proponents of landscape in the Anglo-Saxon world, Geoffrey Jellicoe and John Brinckerhoff Jackson. After specifying such authorial filiation, Cosgrove talks about his ideological debt ("to theorize the *idea* of landscape within a broadly Marxian understanding of culture and society"[13]) and continues, self-quoting, with an extract of his own text "that has been more widely quoted than any other in the book":

> The landscape idea represents a way of seeing—a way in which some Europeans have represented to themselves and to others the world around them and their relationship with it, and through which they have commented on social relations. Landscape is a way of seeing that has its own history, but a history that can be understood only as part of a wider history of economy and society; that has its own assumptions and consequences, but assumptions and consequences whose origins and implications extend well beyond the use and perception of land; that has its own techniques of expression, but techniques which it shares with other areas of cultural practice[14].

Displaying his thought like a billboard in which to condense his own theories after a long "journey" through indicates again, independently of more specifically technical aspects, the autonomy of a pseudo-scientific discourse, happy to talk about its own talking about landscape. Referring to his theory, Cosgrove highlights:

> I am naturally delighted that it has attracted such attention, both within my own discipline and beyond, in anthropology, archaeology, art history and landscape architecture, and also that, through the book's translation into Italian [...], it has engaged with traditions of landscape design and interpretation very different from those of the Anglophone world[15].

While the theory presented by Cosgrove in 1984 reduced landscape to an epiphenomenon—explaining it as the expression of socio-economic changes and revisions of social relations in general—, the

12. D. Cosgrove, *Social Formation and Symbolic Landscape,* Wisconsin University Press, Madison 1998, xiii.
13. *Ibid.*
14. *Ibid.*, xiv.
15. *Ibid.*

4 René Magritte, *The Waterfall* (*La cascade*), 1961

introductory essay of 1998 takes a step forward, defining landscape altogether as a large text: "Introducing the *Iconography of Landscape* Stephen Daniels and I claimed that from today's perspective landscape resembles 'a flickering text displayed on a screen whose meaning can be created, extended, altered, elaborated and finally obliterated by the merest touch of a button"[16].

The revised theory, therefore, forges the myth of a significant progress[17] even there, where it presents a critical or deconstructed interpretation of landscape. Cosgrove's is the perfect example for this practice, since in an act of self-criticism he reprimands his older theory (he began, in 1984, with criticizing the Eurocentric concept of landscape) for having omitted the colonialist, gender ed and non-visual aspects. In 1998, Cosgrove dismantles his previous hypothesis, that is

16. *Ibid.*, xxiv.
17. See A. Roger, *La théorie du paysage en France*, 5-6: "faire avancer la théorie du Paysage", "enrichissement du champ réflexif", "interdisciplinarité vivace" etc.

the creation of a modern identity based on the "figure of the individual European male, conceived as a universal subject, exercising rational self-consciousness within a largely disembodied mind, and endowed with a will to power"[18].

The effort of self-criticism to which Cosgrove submits his thought indicates the basic difficulty related to the very concept of a theory of landscape, and of a theoretical point of view in general. What is at stake behind the correct definition of landscape—and it is, once again, Cosgrove again who reveals it, almost at the expense of landscape itself—is the status of "theory" in the human sciences altogether. This question generated a series of Eurocentric post-idealist narratives that insisted on the death of the subject, the importance of "difference", the free fluctuation of meanings, etc.

Already in 1913, the German philosopher and sociologist Georg Simmel published a short text, *The Philosophy of Landscape* (*Philosophie der Landschaft*), which continues to mark, in a more or less subterranean manner, the contemporary approaches of the phenomenon[19]. In his seminal essay, arguably more poetical than technical, tropisms abound. Simmel resorts often to *enumeratio* ("trees and water-courses, meadows and cornfields"[20]) and hyperbole ("myriad changes in light and clouds"[21]), and he employs a great number of metaphors ("the uninterrupted creation and destruction of forms, the flowing unity of an event"[22]) in order to more closely define his topic. His style combines Nietzschean emphasis ("tragedy of the spirit"[23]) with the post-Romantic figure of the indescribable: "However, the subliminal formula that generates landscape as such cannot be evidenced in an equally simple way, and in principle may not be so at all."[24] While trying to elaborate precise definitions of landscape:

> We say that a landscape arises when a range of natural phenomena spread over the surface of the earth is comprehended by a particular kind of unity, one that is distinct from the way this same visual field is encompassed by the causally thinking scholar, the

---

18. D. Cosgrove, *Social Formation*, xxiv.
19. G. Simmel, *Philosophie der Landschaft*, in «Die Güldenkammer», 1913, II, 635-644 (transl.: *The Philosophy of Landscape*, in «Theory, Culture and Society», December 2007, vol. 24 (7-8), 20-29).
20. *Ibid.*, 636.
21. *Ibid.*, in German: «*tausendfältigen* Wechsel des Lichtes».
22. *Ibid.*, 636-637.
23. *Ibid.*, 637.
24. *Ibid.*, 638.

religious sentiments of a worshipper of nature, the teleologically oriented tiller of the soil, or a strategist of war.[25]

He nevertheless loses control of the scientific argumentation (the emphatic style of his prose recalls of the great German Romantic writer Jean-Paul Richter), drifting more and more towards the concept of atmosphere (*Stimmung*), essential to the final part of his essay:

> When we refer to the mood [*Stimmung*] of a person, we mean that coherent ensemble that either permanently or temporarily colours the entirety of his or her psychic constituents. It is not itself something discrete, and often also not an attribute of any one individual trait. All the same, it is that commonality where all these individual traits interconnect. In the same way, the mood [*Stimmung*]of a landscape permeates all its separate components, frequently without it being attributable to any one of them. In a way that is difficult to specify, each component partakes in it, but a mood prevails which is neither external to these constituents, nor is it composed of them[26].

In Simmel's brilliant sketch one can find, beyond the topical image of the aesthetically insensitive farmer, the majority of topics, images and concepts discussed in the successive theoretical works of his followers (Erwin Straus[27], Henri Maldiney, Manfred Smuda[28], etc.).

Another way to connect a founding philosophical essay via intertextuality to other sources is shown in Rosario Assunto's essay *Metaspazialità del paesaggio*[29]. The author builds his argument starting with the lexicographic analysis of three Italian dictionaries from which emerges a meaning of landscape as "a whole country or part of it, since it has been chosen to be depicted in a painting"[30]. Based on a quick textual analysis, the landscape appears to be the "visual aspect of the country" or, better, "the country considered from the artistic point of view"[31]. Later, Assunto examines the definition of "country" and broadens the linguistic field including definitions from an old edition

---

25. *Ibid.*, 642.
26. *Ibid.*
27. J.-M. Besse, *Voir la terre. Six essais sur le paysage et sur la géographie*, Actes Sud, Arles 2000, 121.
28. M. Smuda, *Landschaft,* Suhrkamp, Frankfurt am Main 1986 (for Flach, 17; for Smuda, 49).
29. R. Assunto, *Il paesaggio e l'estetica*, Aesthetica, Palermo 1994, 19-37.
30. *Ibid.*, 19.
31. *Ibid.*, 21.

of the small and very popular Larousse ("Landscape: extension of the country, *Country*: a *land* that presents an overall view") and from the Dictionary of the *Encyclopœdia Britannica* ("Landscape, 1. A portion of territory that can be viewed at one time from one place")[32]. In the search for the essence of landscape, the philosopher approaches the concept on the basis of documents, which refer to the use of words:

> But our problem, here, is not lexicographic, rather, it is properly philosophic: it is the problem of defining the essence of landscape, its meaning and value to man; and the lexicological moment can only be, if not initial, preliminary to our research: preliminary and useful, valuable perhaps, since it has allowed us to move to the study that concerns us—which is no longer of a terminological kind, but conceptual—after learning that landscape is, according to the dictionaries, a more or less large territory, as it appears to the sight, becoming the object (at least potentially) of a pictorial representation[33].

The status of the scientific discourse that concerns landscape appears therefore problematic. Talking about landscape in a scientific way is often confusing (the protagonists, actually, do not communicate much) and repetitive (they copy abundantly). Drawing inspiration from others, and constructing one's own theoretical system like a piece of fiction seems to be the standard in the field of landscape.

One could, of course, try to summarize the points of view of various protagonists, the position of Jay Appleton for instance, who stresses the biological foundation of landscape (environments allow the survival of species and individuals, even though they also are the objects of aesthetic pleasure[34]. Or we could refer to Stephen Daniels, who considers landscape as fundamentally ambiguous, as a source

---

32. *Ibid.*
33. *Ibid.*, 22.
34. "Aesthetic satisfaction, experienced in the contemplation of landscape, stems from the spontaneous perception of landscape features which, in their shapes, colours, spatial arrangements and other visible attributes, act as sign-stimuli indicative of environmental conditions favourable to survival" (J. Appleton, *The Experience of Landscape,* Wiley, Londonb 1975, 69). Appleton's position reminds of Burke's, when comparing the interest in beauty to the sexual pleasure of procreation (see E. Burke, *A Philosophical Enquiry into the Origin of Our Ideas of the Sublime and Beautiful,* 1759, reprint The Scholar Press, Menston 1970, 63-59).

5 René Magritte, *The Chair* (*La chaise*), 1951

of aesthetic pleasure on the one hand and as a tool of power on the other[35]; or to Augustin Berque and his four criteria of a landscape civilization: linguistic representation, pictorial representation, literary representation, and the art of gardening[36]. Or one could try to grasp further premises, for example the role of Kant, Schiller, Schelling or Humboldt in the genesis of the landscape theories of the twentieth-century.

This study does not allow for an in-depth analysis of filiations, influences and hidden references in the theoretical field. The *talking-about-landscape* however is not limited to the scientific discourse; it has long since entered daily life and verbal routine. The peculiar form of the use of the word "landscape" and its derivatives is the object of Gerhardt Hard's book *Die «Landschaft» der Sprache und die «Landschaft» der Geographen*[37]. In summary, Hard highlights:

> (True) landscape is vast and harmonious, quiet, colorful, large, varied and beautiful. It is mainly an aesthetical phenomenon, closer to the eye than the reason, more related to heart, soul, sensitivity and its dispositions rather than spirit and intellect, closer to the female principle rather than the male one. True landscape is the result of a becoming, something organic and living. It is more familiar than foreign, but farther than closer, it expresses more nostalgia than presence; it elevates us above everyday life and adjoins poetry. But, even though it refers to something unlimited, infinite, maternal landscape also always offers man a homeland, warmth and shelter. It is a treasure of the past, of history, culture and tradition, of peace and freedom, happiness and love, of the rest in the countryside, of solitude and health, recovered in relation to the frenzy of daily life and the noise of the city; one must cross it and live it on foot because it will not reveal its secret to the tourist or the bare intellect[38].

---

35. S. Daniels, *Fields of Vision: Landscape Imagery and National Identity in England and the United States*, Cambridge University Press, Cambridge 1993.
36. See A. Berque, *Les raisons du paysage. De la Chine antique aux environnements de synthèse*, Hazan, Paris 1995.
37. G. Hard, *Die «Landschaft» der Sprache und die «Landschaft» der Geographen. Semantische und forschungslogische Studien*, Ferd Dümmlers Verlag, Bonn 1970.
38. *Ibid.*, 20-21.

The scenario outlined by Hard reveals that the word "landscape" belongs to a specific linguistic system of great complexity. The use of the term is, invariably, accompanied by typical epithets[39]. The *talking-about-landscape* in daily life is never neutral. It is, rather, inscribed in a specific linguistic context, national—at first—, regional, and individual. Typical German semantic associations, such as the untranslatable concept of *Stimmung*, which we have already encountered, meaning something more than mere "atmosphere", that of *Sehnsucht* (more than just "longing"), or other terms closer to the irrational, like *Gemüt, Herz* ("heart"), or Seele ("soul"), can prove this. Ideological categories such as *Heimat* ("homeland") or *Tradition* also influence the perception of landscape.

Both the scholarly and the everyday approach lead, as a last consequence, to the question: to what extent do the words used to label landscape mark, or even create the phenomenon to which they refer? It is a problem that interferes with the question of the primacy of language over thought, attributable to Wilhelm von Humboldt: "Landscape is thus, at least on the level of the senses, the means through which man, and the world in which he lives, take shape"[40]. Humboldt, who considered language as a "formative organ of thought"[41] and as *energeia*, identified the plurality of national languages as just as many sources of visions of the world (*Weltansichten*). The Humboldtian idea lives on in the Sapir-Whorf hypothesis. According to Edward Sapir, we are "at the mercy of the social patterns called words"[42]. Or, as his disciple Benjamin Lee Whorf put it: "We dissect nature along lines laid down by our native languages"[43]. To possess or not to possess the words to define landscape acquires then, as Augustin Berque highlights[44], a fundamental importance. Even the possibility to translate European words or to impose them, as well as the ease in coining neologisms based on the suffix "-*scape*", is not a negligible fact.

Whether agreeing with Sapir and Whorf on the linguistic creation of the world as such, or 'relativizing' such a position on the basis of

39. *Ibid.*,18-19.
40. Letter to F. Schiller, quoted in J. Trabant, *Traditionen Humboldts*, Suhrkamp, Frankfurt am Main 1990, 38.
41. *Ibid.*
42. E. Sapir, *The Status of Linguistics as a Science*, in «Language», December 1929, 5, 4, 207-214, in particular 209.
43. B. Whorf, *Language, Thought and Reality*, MIT Press, Cambridge Mass. 1956, 212.
44. See Berque, *Les raisons du paysage*.

the interaction of language with psychological or social factors, the use of everyday terms to designate landscape necessarily refers to an interpretative act. Landscape is, in other words, always mediated by the terms we use in order to define it, from the private sphere of the individual, to the semi-private, semi-public sphere of the scientific discourse, to the public realm of official "definitions", for instance in legal texts. The discourse on landscape, after having been confined for a long time to the happy few, to the Ruskins and Rudorffs[45] and to their ideology, has reached after a century of "progress" in terms of the visibility of the phenomenon at the 20th century political and legal consecration.

The most recent and important document, the *European Landscape Convention*, raises, however, independently of the mere fact of its existence, a number of interrogations. The *Convention* frequently mingles landscape as a cultural phenomenon with landscape as an environmental phenomenon. It uses vague formulas open to extremely subjective interpretations (how to understand "quality" in the formula: "the public's wish to enjoy high quality landscapes", quoted in the *Preamble* of the *Convention*?), and it puts forward equivocal categories such as the creation of landscapes (who can really create a landscape?) or "landscape management" (we can manage a territory, a site, a region, etc. – but landscape?). And what should we think of the following statement: "Landscape must become a mainstream political concern, since it plays an important role in the well-being of Europeans who are no longer prepared to tolerate the alteration of their surroundings by technical and economic developments in which they have no say"[46], as it is contradicted by the *Preamble* of the very same *Convention*, which speaks of identification of landscape as "a resource favorable to economic activity"?

---

45. See F. Walter, *Les figures paysagères de la Nation: territoire et paysage en Europe*, EHESS, Paris 2004.

46. *Explanatory Report to the European Landscape Convention*, Council of Europe, n. 23, 2000.

CHAPTER III

FOR A DEFINITION
OF LANDSCAPE

How to Define Landscape

After highlighting these fundamental difficulties, it is necessary to outline the conditions of possibility for a definition of landscape. Every attempt to situate landscape, whether based on theoretical reflection or starting from the practice of everyday language, will necessarily face a series of founding paradoxes.

The first difficulty could be thusly formulated: landscape is never a fact; it is not something measurable or identifiable, but is a phenomenon that avoids any attempt of being defined in purely objective terms. Landscape is not the land, nor the country or the site. Hence the problematic issue of its representation. Both iconic and verbal representations (transcriptions and descriptions)—as well as individual and empirical representations, the impression that we have create of a landscape at a given time—clash with the open, fluctuant identity of the phenomenon. In his *Notebooks,* the English Romantic poet Coleridge highlights the endless work which an adequate transcription of landscape would require:

> The Head of Glen Nevish how simple for a Painteri/& in how many words & how laboriously—in what dim similitudes & slow & dragging Circumlocutions must I give it—so give it that who knew the place best would least recognize it in my description[1].

In his already cited *Philosophy of Landscape*, Georg Simmel appropriately speaks of landscape as a "work of art in *statu nascendi*"[2]. A further paradox results from the double use of the same term. When using the term "landscape", in many European languages, we designate both a representation—the painting, the photograph, the work of art—and a mental phenomenon, that is, in the here and now, presented to someone *as* landscape. Yet, is it possible to observe or to contemplate a landscape without already reproducing, consciously or unconsciously, pre-existent models or patterns? 'Real' landscape, the one discovered on site, is in other terms actually a representation of a representation. The Japanese

---

1. *The Notebooks of Samuel Taylor Coleridge*, ed. K. Coburn, Routledge & Kegan Paul, London 1957, note 1489.
2. G. Simmel, *Philosophie der Landschaft*, in «Die Güldenkammer», 1913, II, 635-644 (transl.: *The Philosophy of Landscape*, in «Theory, Culture and Society», December 2007, vol. 24 (7-8), 20-29).

6 Katshushika Hokusai, **Red Fuji**, in *Thirty-six views of Mount Fuji* (1829-1831)

writer Dazai Osamu, in his short story *One Hundred Views of Mount Fuji*, has illustrated the difficulties in overcoming the dizzying contradictions of landscape representations. How could one not find Mount "beautiful", since the Japanese culture never ceased to produce literary and artistic images of the national mountain? But how can it be considered "beautiful", given that, even compared to the most standardized representations, the real landscape of Mount Fuji will only rarely be able to surprise us? Osamu, aware of this dilemma, tells the story of a disenchantment, an actual deconstruction of Mount Fuji.

> If I were living in India, for example, and were suddenly snatched up and carried off by an eagle and dropped on the beach at Numazu in Japan, I doubt if I'd be very much impressed at the sight of this mountain. Japans "Fujiyama" is "wonderful" to foreigners simply because they've heard so

much about it and yearned so long to see it; but how much appeal would Fuji hold for one who has never been exposed to such popular propaganda, for one whose heart is simple and pure and free of preconceptions? It would, perhaps, strike that person as almost pathetic, as mountains go. It's short, really. In relation to the width of its base, quite short. Any mountain with a base that size should be at least half again as tall[3].

Hence, it is only a radically unusual point of view that provides the expected encounter with Mount Fuji. "At dawn I went to relieve myself, and through the wire mesh screen covering the square window in the toilet I could see Fuji. Small, pure white, leaning slightly to the left: that's one Fuji I'll never forget."[4] Dazai's ironic perspective, the view through the bathroom window, demonstrates both the impossibility of a landscape to be given as such and forever and the possibility, in certain circumstances, to still be surprised by it. It also shows the extent to which the sudden appearance reveals a complex cultural construction. Landscape is the artificial, the unnatural result of a culture that perpetually redefines its relationship with nature. This reminds us of another significant paradox: the experience of landscape is, generally and in the first place, an experience of the self. When we are touched by a landscape, the object discovered is essential, but the act of perceiving as such is equally important. The beholder is entirely part of the landscape which he creates. Hence, the fundamental *non-identity* of landscape, its being part of a history (the history of landscape), which could be defined as the history of the consciousness of landscape. Landscape exists only as consciousness; it actually *is* (in) this consciousness.

Our explanation does not solve the already announced confusion between the two distinct realities indicated by the same term, "landscape". We use "landscape" with reference to a certain type of images, that is artistic representation, and we refer it at the same time to something we see in space, to a 'real' landscape perceived from a "Here-I-Now" (Moles). Now, the most relevant

---

3. D. Osamu, *Fugaku Hyakkey* (transl.: *One Hundred Views of Mount Fuji*, in *Run, Melos! And other stories,* ed. Ralph F. McCarthy, Kodansha International, Tokyo 1988, 12).
4. *Ibid.*, 13.

paradox concerning landscape consists of the historical fact that the artistic representation[5] precedes the mental representation. Landscape, at first, was nothing but a particular type of painting, an artistic image of a piece of nature, and only much later, thanks to artistic and poetic practice, did landscape become something else, the experience of a part of nature perceived by someone at a glimpse. The history of the French word "paysage" is, from this point of view, revealing. "Paysage", used for the first time around 1500—more precisely in 1493, by the poet Jean Molinet[6]—is a neologism. It is composed of the noun "pays" followed by the suffix "-age", the latter understood as "whole", "overview", "entirety", or "totality" (Simmel recalls this aspect of the experience of landscape when writing of "a self-contained perception intuited as a self-sufficient unity"[7]), just as in the French word "feuillage" (foliage)[8]. Whether the word "paysage" originates in the Dutch term "landschap"[9] or in other sources is of lesser importance than the unquestionable fact of its invention and imposition. "Paysage", just as "paesaggio" (in Italy the word appears for the first time with Vasari, around 1550) or "paisaje", is a verbal artefact for a new reality, while other expressions belonging to the European languages such as "landscape", "Landschaft", or "landschap"—which would later take on, at least partly, an aesthetic connotation—are pre-existent (they designate the region, the area, the homeland, and even the population)[10]. In the Renaissance, "paysage" refers to a picture that represents nature, or to a pictorial genre in which the representation of nature is highly important, to the point that it justifies the use of a new technical term.

5. For the lexicographic importance of the representation see F.-P. Tourneux, *De l'espace vu au tableau ou les définitions du mot paysage dans les dictionnaires de langue française du XVIIe au XIXe siècles*, in *La théorie du paysage en France 1794-1994*, 203.
6. See J.-P. Le Dantec, *Jardins et paysage: une anthologie*, Larousse, Paris 1996, 93.
7. Simmel, *Philosophie der Landschaft*, 639.
8. J. Martinet, *Paysage: signifiant et signifié*, in *Lire le paysage, lire les paysages*, CIEREC, Saint-Etienne 1983, 62.
9. See A. Roge, *Court traité du paysage*, Gallimard, Paris 1997; C. Franceschi, *Du mot paysage et de ses équivalents dans cinq langues européennes*, in *Les enjeux du paysage*, ed.:M. Collot, Ousia, Bruxelles 1997, 75-111.
10. See R. Gruenter, *Landschaft. Bemerkungen zur Wort- und Bedeutungsgeschichte*, in *Landschaft und Raum in der Erzählkunst*, ed.: A. Ritter, WBG, Darmstadt 1975.

The form of the French word, moreover, suddenly reveals, and this time in accordance with the other European languages which possess a similar term, the non-identity, too often forgotten, of the "land" and the "landscape". The landscape includes the land, but something else, designated by the suffix "-age" ["-scape", in English], overlaps, takes control of the view of it. The suffix clearly hints to the fact that we are dealing with an element added to the land, hence, that it is a particular point of view that determines landscape. Jeanne Martinet has linked the etymology of "pays"—through lat. *pagus, pagensis*[11]—to the verb "pango", to plant a pole. A "pays", land, is a marked territory, an identification based on the founding action of the hand of man, which generates, at the same time, an original spatiality[12]. By now, it is possible to suggest a heuristic definition of landscape based on what has been previously discussed. It can take an extended narrative form, for instance: "landscape is a stretch of country encompassed by the gaze of the subject" or "landscape is a slice of an area that can be perceived at a glance." We propose, instead as a practical reminder a short formula:

$$L = S + N$$

Landscape refers—it appears obvious from this formula—to three essential factors, or *sine qua non* conditions:
1: a subject (no landscape without a subject)
2: nature (no landscape without nature)
3: a relationship between the two, subject and nature, indicated by the symbol "+" (no landscape without connection, bond or encounter *between* subject and nature).

The role of the subject

The subject represents the first and essential element in the existence of landscape. By subject we mean an individual provided with subjectivity, namely a human being who stands out thanks to

---

11. See Martinet, *Paysage: signifiant et signifié*, in: *Lire le paysage, lire les paysages*, 62.
12. See Yi Fu Tuan, *Space and Place: The Perspective of Experience*, Arnold, London 1977.
13. «*Subject*, in the philosophical language, starting from the seventeenth century, means the individual, the *ego* who considers what surrounds him as an *object*» (J. Ritter, *Subjektivität und industrielle Gesellschaft*, in Id., *Subjektivität. Sechs Aufsätze,* Suhrkamp, Frankfurt am Main 1974, 11).

his peculiar *being-in-the-world*.[13] Another way to characterize this person is with his identification as "modern" subject, subjectivity and modernity referring both to a historical moment and to an attitude or disposition. Being the subject of modernity implies a separation or a break with the pastidentified by Simmel as the "dissolution of primordial ligatures"[14]—the idea of the loss of a previous state and the debut of a new era, precisely the modern one. Subjectivity and modernity imply surpassing a threshold[15], the beginning of a founding crisis.

It is possible to imagine this transformation into a subject in analogy with the psychogenesis of the child who turns into an adolescent: becoming a subject represents an awakening for the human being, accompanied by the pain for the irreparable loss of a state marked by non-difference, in short, by pre-reflective unity. The crisis frees the subject at the cost, of course, of the awareness of the definitive loss of the previous condition.

A socio-historical explanation, like the one Norbert Elias makes, by referring to the development of a differentiated society which results from the "civilizing process", is another possibility to clarify modernity. We can try to contextualize the genesis of subjectivity by referening to socio-economic factors as well, for example following Denis Cosgrove who, in 1984, argued for the replacement of "use-values" with "exchange-values" as for the transition from feudalism to capitalism[16]. From this angle, the development of subjectivity or modernity no longer concerns only the life of the individual, but that of a community, which evolves or emancipates itself in a certain historical period.

Talking about modernity implies, at any rate, the danger of including and legitimizing the concept at the basis of the very movement that has invented and imposed it on posterity. In other words, modernity and subjectivity are the flagships of a dominant discourse that is shaken by deconstructivist critique from head to foot. During the twentieth-century, the "subject" has been made fragile, placed in brackets, beheaded. Deconstruction has sentenced its death and declared the extreme vulnerability of the "heroic" or "bourgeois" model.

14. Simmel, *Philosophie der Landschaft*, 637.
15. See M. Jakob, *L'émergence du paysage*, Infolio, Gollion 2004.
16. D. Cosgrove, *Social Formation and Symbolic Landscape*, xi.

At the end of a ruthless dismantling process, subjectivity appears as nothing more than an illusion, and, at most, as a former construction now outdated. In addition, subjectivity was identified as a typical representation or forced imposition—claimed to be *the* truth—of an ideological point of view. Should we then talk of subjectivity, modernity, and of a dominant, if not imperialist ideology, culminating with the imposition of landscape, as William J. T. Mitchell suggested in *Landscape and Power*? "At a minimum we need to explore the possibility that the representation of landscape is not only a matter of internal politics and national or class ideology but also an international, global phenomenon, intimately bound up with the discourse of imperialism."[17] Critical philosophy intended in a broad sense (from analytic philosophy of language to the Frankfurt School and post-structuralism) suggests a careful and dual approach to the history of the subject. When considering the subject, we have to be as precise as possible and redefine our conceptual frame in the light of the most recent theoretical explanations of the phenomenon. Dealing with landscape in the context of subjectivity, we exceed the boundaries of the question and we are confronted to fundamental questions of philosophy in general. We propose, however, not to enter the endless debate linked to subjectivity in general, but to outline relevant aspects of modernity and subjectivity starting *from* landscape. In other words, landscape appears as a paradigm of modernity, and it is thanks to landscape—an intimately subjective experience—that subjectivity can be explained and understood in more adequate terms. The conquest of an elevated point of view represents one of these aspects related both to the "rise" of landscape and of subjectivity. The development of landscape conscience corresponds with a historical perspective to the occupation of a height, an elevation that is physical, symbolic, and transcendental. Petrarch, the "first modern man" (Jacob Burckhardt), handed down an exceptional document of this founding act in his letter known as *The Ascent of Mont Ventoux*. Francesco recounts how he climbed the highest mountain of the region motivated by curiosity (a capital sin), that is the desire to look down at the world below. For him, the mountain peak worked as a platform of elevation on different levels.

17. W.J.T. Mitchell, **Landscape and Power,** The University of Chicago Press, Chicago/London 2002.

7 Vaucluse, anonymous etching, 17th century

As a "new" man, the humanist and poet distances himself, in an act of conscious transgression, from the normative precepts of theology. The modern subject trespasses the rules of the plain, of an imposed flat life, rising with his own strengths and will to the top, where he experiences a surprising sight:

> First of all, moved by a certain accustomed quality of the air and by the unrestricted spectacle, I stood there as in a trance. I looked back. Clouds were beneath me. And suddenly what I had heard and read about Athos and Olympus became less incredible to me when I looked out from this mountain of lesser fame. I then directed my sight toward Italy[18].

However the act that elevates Petrarch to the top of self-determination is, at the same time, mimetic; it is the remake of an imperial gesture: that of princes, strategists and great men of this world, who were able to project themselves to the same heights in the past[19]. The

---

18. *Ibid.*, 9.
19. F. Petrarca, *La lettera del Ventoso—Familiarum Rerum Libri, IV, I*, ed. M. Formica, M. Jakob, Tararà, Verbania 1997, §§ 17-18 (*The Ascent of Mont Ventoux* in *Letters on Familiar Matters—Rerum familiarum libri, 4, 1*, translated by A. S. Bernarndo, John Hopkins University Press, Baltimore 1982.)

subject on the top momentarily distances himself symbolically from his former naïve, pre-subjective life and faces the open perspective of discovery; now he is able to project himself not only with his mind, but also visually into an open space. Petrarch leaves, with his most famous letter, a written trace of this adventure, and in his case the adventure is, mainly, writing. The experience at the top of Mont Ventoux has important chorographic and scopic implications. The impression Petrarch leaves to posterity, that of the lone observer on the highest possible point of view, hints already at the later development of modern spatiality. The new subject, self-conscious and in an elevated position, is free in his movements (Petrarch is a keen traveler, a pre-Romantic wayfarer who clambers a mountain "led solely by a desire to view the great height of it"[20]), a freedom that he can also exercise by mentally projecting himself towards farther areas: "the Alps themselves, frozen and snow-covered, through which that wild enemy of the Roman people once crossed and, if we believe the story, broke its way through the rocks with vinegar, seemed very close to me, although separated by a great distance"[21]. The disposition illustrated by Petrarch is based on the empirical knowledge of the world, on the thirst for space to which, at the same time, it contributes. His stance on the top of Mont Ventoux has another quality worthy of attention: the act of simultaneously being close to the world (seen) and to put it at the right distance in order to be grasped. At first, the new perspective with its unusual sight causes, literally, a sense of vertigo. The initial physical malaise and uncertainty ("I stood there as in a trance", or better even: "I stood there blocked in stupor"[22]) as well as the feeling of absolute immobility will leave room, once the eye regains all of its organizing force, to the "landscapes" evoked by the narrator.

The subject is the one who has the world *before* his eyes, *in front* of him. By occupying this position, he immediately experiences himself as the *other* of the world. The correct distance acts, here, as the condition of visibility and, at the same time, it is cause for surprise. The visual conquest suggests a potentially limitless

---

20. See *ibid.*, §2 (Philip II of Macedon's ascent of Mount Haimos).
21. *Ibid.*, § 1.
22. *Ibid.*, § 18.

freedom—the subject's freedom of action[23]—giving this act the quality of an initial discovery. The desire to increase his knowledge, to appropriate the world, so palpable in Petrarch's life and writings, has, both structurally and symbolically, its origin in this new *position*. The Mont Ventoux episode, whether real or only imagined, represents an absolute starting point and a point of no return. It is starting from this highest of all possible points of view that the (re-) appropriation of the world begins. With Petrarch debuts the history of the subject, subjectivity *in progress*. It will later take countless shapes and paths, more or less intimately bound with landscape. The history of the gaze, the history of the conquest of nature, of perspective, self-consciousness and consciousness of the history of art as history of the landscape genre are all the expression and the ground of subjectivity.

For the subject, the history of art is far from being a mere intellectual or artistic means. Art is, on the contrary, the place where the subject is aesthetically formatted or educated—in the strong sense of the term. One good example for the relations between artistic practice and subjectivity is one-point perspective, whose history touches that of landscape without completely crossing it. Landscape shares the importance of spaces and horizons with mathematical perspective. One-point perspective allows, once assimilated and applied, to visualize space thanks to the new images of the world identified as "landscapes". One-point perspective is based, it is well known, on a fictional monocular gaze[24]; it corresponds to the ideal of a homogeneous space given to a single and static eye. The fixity of the central point of view that presupposes the presence of an almighty eye clearly anticipates the heroic subject of idealistic philosophy, the absolute subjectivity. The history of the landscape genre corrects, starting from the moment in which it connects with one-point perspective, the exclusive fiction, by confronting the arti-

---

23. *Ibid.*, § 20.
24. "Beyond the freedom of contemplation, but already in the contemplation that sees the landscape as an horizon of freedom, the freedom becomes aware of itself as an indeterminate and unconditioned possibility of doing [...] In the landscape, the man discovers thus his own freedom as a freedom of nature with which—in the aesthetic contemplation—he feels identified; but the consciousness of this freedom of his makes him, so to speak, divorce nature" (R. Assunto, *Il paesaggio e l'estetica*, 359-360).

ficial gaze with the observed perceptual space. The "fabricated" gaze (Cassirer) of one-point perspective, a point of view that is neither natural nor spontaneous, will be subjected, over the centuries, to the increasing competition of the mobile, bi-ocular eye of the empirical perception.

Landscape is caught in the grips of artifice and personal perception. In the beginning, it is nothing else (the history of the word clearly shows it) than an artistic representation or, in Roger de Piles' words: "Landscape is a genre of painting that represents the countryside and the objects that can be found in it"[25]. Now, a painting is, by nature, non-narrative, fixed, static; it feigns a stalemate which the observer must find again and recreate, in order to be apprehended correctly. The logic operating in one-point perspective, mathematical-scopic logic, guides the construction of the landscape-image as much as its reception. Both demand control and dominance on space. The strong repression of another, more instinctive logic—the corporal one of a subject who permanently displaces himself and creates the reality based on his somatic perspective—will be recovered in landscape. The history of landscape as a pictorial genre appears then as a long, intense, cultural work in progress, an epistemological endeavor that, applied on real scenery, allows the creation of landscapes as purely mental representations on site.

---

25. See E. Panofsky, *Perspective as Symbolic Form*, Zone Books, New York 1991; S. Edgerton, *The Renaissance Rediscovery of Linear Perspective*, Basic Books, New York 1975; L. Schmeiser, *Die Erfindung der Zentralperspektive und die Entstehung der neuzeitlichen Wissenschaft*, Fink, Munich 2002.

Nature in sight

If the phenomenon of landscape is not to be taken for granted, this applies to nature as well. There are many reasons which explain nature's invisibility. Nature can historically be absent because of its negativity, or simply because it is feared[26]. For centuries, at least in Europe, nature was globally perceived as a place of perdition, as the devil's dominion. The idea of *natura lapsa*[27], nature consubstantially marked by the fall of man, has given rise to the powerful imagination of a post-deluge world, where everything wild and untamed appeared as irreparably negative. Starting from the fourth-century A.C., with the Church Fathers, this line of thought has continued—in spite of the continuous developments of theology and the partial criticisms levelled against it—to influence the minds until the seventeenth-century. Nature was meant, at best, as a gift from the Creator to his unworthy creature while, at worst, it took the ill-fated appearance of the *mundus senescens*[28], of a *locus terribilis* profoundly luciferian. The most influent invectives against the *voluptas* or the *concupiscentia oculorum* can be found in the *Confessions* of Saint Augustine, where even the most innocent gaze on the natural world is severely condemned:

> When I am sitting at home and a lizard is catching flies or a spider is trapping them as they blunder into its web, how often does this catch my attention! Is the activity any different, merely because the animals are small? From these incidents I advance to praising you, O wondrous creator and orderer of all things, but I did not begin by being concerned with this. It is one thing to rise quickly, another thing not to fall[29].

The power of this strong religious filter has not only contributed to the nearly complete oblivion of classical theories regarding

---

26. R. de Piles, *Cours de peinture par principes,* J. Estienne, Paris 1708, 200.
27. On the ambiguity of nature see A.O. Lovejoy, «Nature» as Aesthetic Norm, in Id., *Essays in the History of Ideas*, The Johns Hopkins University Press, Baltimore 1948, 76.
28. See D. Groh, *Schöpfung im Widerspruch. Deutungen der Natur und des Menschen von der Genesis bis zur Reformation,* Suhrkamp, Frankfurt am Main 2003, 17 ss.
29. See Lucretius, *De rerum natura*, II, 1144 ss.

nature—including the empirical knowledge derived from observation—but also to a generalized blindness towards nature as such. Forgetting nature implied, at the same time, the need to symbolically overcome it: the profane signs of the earthly world had to be read in light of the sacred text, transposed on a level of "deep" signification that explained the sense of the sublunary phenomena[30]. The theologian Johann Arndt clearly states it:

> So, in short, we may consider all things as upbraiding us with our iniquities, and warning us to repent. What is the *thunder*, but the terrible voice of heaven, at which the earth trembles, and by which God speaks to the impenitent world? What is an earthquake, but a lecture of repentance?[31]

Another filter, both anthropological and psychological, is due to the fact that to venture out of the village or the city and to go beyond the rural boundaries (to leave an already-domesticated nature) *towards* or *inside* nature, involved actual dangers everywhere. The religious interpretation identified these far-away places, forests, mountains, and deserted areas as real allegories of the separation from God, of sin and guilty solitude. Let us not forget that curiosity had been considered a deadly sin for a long time.

In order for nature to turn, from unknown and feared, into a safe and known place (the allegory of the *Securitas* watching over the «good» territory, in the famous fresco of Siena), a long cultural work has been necessary[32]. This, during the post-Dantesque period and more precisely near the end of the Middle Ages—let alone practical forays like deforestation[33]—takes the form of a pre-

---

30. See Augustinus, *Confessiones*, X, 35-37 (transl.: *The Confessions of St. Augustine*, Image Books, New York 1960).
31. See C. Begemann, *Furcht und Angst im Prozeß der Aufklärung*, Suhrkamp, Frankfurt am Main 1987, 70 ss.
32. J. Arndt, *Sämtliche Geistreiche Bücher vom Wahren Christentum*, Frankfurt am Main 1715, p. 908 (transl.: *True Christianity*, Smith, English & Co., Philadelphia 1868).
33. The history of architecture supplies a clear evidence of this anthropological fear of nature: "one must not forget that all of man's purposes are aspects of one fundamental purpose: to defend ourselves from danger, to find a remedy against the horrors of life, to save ourselves from pain and death. To build a shelter against the inclemency of the weather and the threats of wild beasts and enemies—to build a home—is one of the most ancient forms of that will of safety" (E. Severino, *Tecnica e architettura*, Cortina, Milan 2003, p. 87).

8 Ambrogio Lorenzetti, *The Allegory of Good and Bad Government*, fresco, around 1350, Siena, Palazzo Pubblico, Sala dei Nove

scientific exploration (of the *tacuini sanitatis* genre), literary texts (poetry, letters, travel literature, etc.) and artistic representation. Petrarch and his coevals left us decisive examples from this point of view. The author of the *Canzoniere* will transform poetry forever, revolutionizing the lyric lexicon through expressions that refer to nature. Words like "rock", "stone", "meadow", "hill", "spring", "torrent", "cloud" etc. changed the poetic language quantitatively and qualitatively. Nature became the main and decisive picture of a subject—no longer only of the figure of the poet—who is reflected in it over and over again. Two verses of *Sonnet XXXV* may be enough to serve as an example of this relation between a self-conscious subject and nature in its most unusual form—that of the desolate country, with no sign of life—around and before him: "Alone and deep in thought I measure out / the most deserted fields, with slow, late steps".

The desire for nature shows through countless of Petrarch's pages. It reveals itself theoretically and poetically and becomes real also in the practice of the "landscape-gardener" who isolates himself in the solitude of *Valchiusa*[34]. This mythical place of poetry and landscape draws the attention on a further aspect of this Petrarchan shelter: the idyll of Vaucluse for Petrarch represents the opposite

34. See C. Glacken, *Traces on the Rhodian Shore. Nature and Culture in the Western Thought from Ancient Times to the End of the Eighteenth Century,* California University Press, Berkeley 1967.

of the city. It is only starting from the city (a place that has lost the symbiotic contact with its surroundings) that consciousness and the desire for nature lead to the creation of landscape. Thus, it is not he who lives directly in or from nature, the shepherd, the farmer or the hunter, who creates the idea of nature, but rather he who is separated from it, the citizen. The consciousness of not being part of nature anymore, of being able to find it only on the outside, *extra muros*, causes at the same time the feeling of alienation characteristic of the urban consciousness and the "solution" of finding a remedy outside the city. Petrarch, the most famous intellectual of his time, is the character who embodies, biographically and semiologically (his actions suddenly become text and image, they are inscribed in a story) the *act of leaving* the city to re-appropriate lost nature.

The separation (*city/non-city, subject/non-subject*), the feeling of malaise and loss are at the basis of these crucial changes. They turn the indifference towards nature into interest in it. Norbert Elias supplies a meaningful description:

> The manner in which *nature* is experienced is fundamentally affected, slowly at the end of the Middle Ages and then more quickly from the sixteenth century onwards, by the pacification of larger and larger populated areas. Only now do forests, meadows and mountains gradually cease to be danger zones of the first order, from which anxiety and fear constantly intrude into individual life. And now, as the network of roads becomes, like social interdependence in general, more dense; as robber-knights and beasts of prey slowly disappear; as forest and field cease to be the scene of unbridled passions, of the savage pursuit of man and beast, of wild joy and wild fear, and as they are moulded by intertwining peaceful activities, the production of goods, trade and transport; now, to pacified people a correspondingly pacified nature becomes visible, and in a new way. It becomes [...] to a high degree an object of visual pleasure. In addition, people—more precisely the townpeople for whom forest and field are no longer their everyday background but a place of relaxation—grow more sensitive and begin to see the open country in a more differentiated way[35].

35. See E. Battisti, *Non chiare acque*, in Id., *Iconologia ed ecologia del giardino e del paesaggio*, Olschki, Florence 2004.

The relationship subject-nature

Subjectivity and consciousness of nature do not ensure by themselves the creation of landscape. The existence of a strong bond between the two is necessary in order to make it possible. Nature has to involve the subject in a specific way and it is only after that relationship has formed that the landscape can exist. He who lives a pre-reflective, mythical relationship with nature, will not have any concept of it. He, being too close to nature, which is omnipresent, will not be able to identify himself as the *other*, the one who is excluded from nature. His attention will almost always be focused on nature, which he will experience both physically and biologically. The problem remains that of getting to know the sites, a task that is carried out by marking paths and naming places, inscribing them in the collective memory[36]. The way through the territory represents, from this point of view, an actual "pedestrian speech act"[37]. The relationship with nature, gradually becoming familiar and controlled, is initially expressed through the signs and the constructions created by man on the territory, and then through agriculture.

The citizen Socrates, who claims, right in the middle of an *extra muros* walk, that he does not learn anything from the open country and the trees[38], is the historical witness (even if relegated to a spokesman of Platonism) of a radical change. Socrates is fully aware of the distance between himself and what surrounds him, namely, nature. This appears to be even more meaningful if we consider that the main theme of pre-Socratic philosophy is, in fact, nature. Thus, it is possible to consult nature theoretically, like Thales, Anaximenes, Anaximander or Empedocles did, without *being in the difference* as far as the belonging to nature itself is concerned. Pre-Socratic theories, even if they deal with nothing else than nature, are not sufficient for the creation of the distance that is necessary to allow another view on nature. The concept of *theoria tou kosmou*, essential to understand nature in Greek philosophy, refers, through the idea of *theoria*, to the visual perception[39]. This, though, is only a transit-point, necessary to access the invisible essence, the intelli-

---

36. N. Elias, *Über den Prozess der Zivilisation*, 405-406.
37. We agree with C. Tilley, *A Phenomenology of Landscape*; what Tilley indicates as "landscape", though, seems to us the "territory" or "country".
38. *Ibid.*, 30.
39. Plato, *Phaedrus*, 230d.

gible world. Any theory of nature worthy of this name transcends therefore the sphere of mere appearance, for an understanding of the cosmic order, the being, the authentic totality of nature. Everything, from plants to animals and human beings, takes part in the intelligence of the cosmos. The Greek thought on nature remains, on closer view, essentialist. It aims, as the different meaning of the word *physis* in Aristotle's *Metaphysics* show, at the genesis, the origin of nature, the original matter, and so on. As for the ancient times in general and the Hellenistic classical period in particular, whether the "subject" existed or not is a controversial question that stands even nowadays[40]. Without considering the lack of an adequate term to designate the subject, and taking into account the Socratic position—that, despite not possessing an equivalent word, did not cease to imply what we call "ego"—we shall ask ourselves if landscape could have existed at the times of Socrates, or right after him. Well, landscape could have been there—in spite of the lack of a word or a description that indicates it—if only Socrates had *wanted* to look at nature, something that, as we know, he refused to do.

Once again, everything leads to believe that greater sociocultural factors—like the development of an actual urban consciousness and the corresponding feeling of alienation and crisis—are necessary for the sophisticated, disenchanted subject (who no longer needs to know nature for purposes of necessity or through tradition) to show interest in it in other ways. The city, the urban whole, in the strong sense of the term, differs completely from the previous dwelling-places. It represents, as Joachim Ritter pointed out, the true origin of freedom and law[41], namely a place in which ideas that are lived and accepted as such impose themselves on reality. However, it works, at least on the level of knowledge, as an increasingly independent social space, separated from the outside. The relationship with nature is no longer, like in the past, already *given*; it has to be reinvented and recreated. The man of the city is, by definition, the man who does not know nature anymore. The practical knowledge, the use of nature, essential for the survival, is not part of his world anymore.

---

40. See J. Ritter, *Landschaft. Zur Funktion des Ästhetischen in der modernen Gesellschaft*, Aschendorf, Münster 1978.
41. See, from this point of view, the nostalgic attempts to recover the ancient landscape in M. Venturi-Ferriolo, *Etiche del paesaggio. Il progetto del mondo umano*, Editori Riuniti, Rome 2002, 35 ss.

Getting nature back means building a relationship on the basis of a loss, a non-belonging. In this case it is neither about the practical knowledge of people "naturally" close to nature (the invention of the idyll in the third-century B.C., with the character of the idealized shepherd, expresses this impossible dream creating the nature-culture hybrid of the intellectual-shepherd), nor about observation or theoretical analysis. The essential happens on a symbolic level; on a level of representation[42]. Since the repossession of nature is a task of the eye, of the gaze of the subject, it becomes real through a vision. Nature becomes image. The image is not that of disparate elements *inside* nature; rather, or especially, it is a global picture, through a unity which designates the totality offering an extract of it, a "piece", a "shred". Or, in Simmel's words, again:

> To talk of a *piece of nature* is in fact a self-contradiction. Nature is not composed of pieces. It is the unity of a whole. The instant anything is parceled out from this wholeness, it is no longer nature pure and simple since this whole can be nature only within that unbounded unity, only as a wave within that total flux. As far as landscape is concerned, however, a boundary, a way of being encompassed by a momentary or permanent field of vision, is quite essential. Its material foundation or its individual pieces may simply be regarded as nature. But conceived of as a 'landscape', it demands a status for itself, which may be optical, aesthetic or mood-centred. There needs to be a unique, characterizing detachment from that indivisible unity of nature in which each piece serves as a transit-point for the totality of the forces of existence[43].

As image or representation of nature, landscape is never a simple *fact*. It resorts to the imagination that creates it (the German word *Einbildungskraft*, the "power of forming images", fittingly conveys

---

42. J. Ritter, *Die große Stadt*, In Id., *Metaphysik und Politik*, Suhrkamp, Frankfurt am Main 2003, pp. 341-354. Ritter refers to the "realization of the *being-man* as a city" and underscores that "philosophy has its place inside the city" (*ibid.*, 350).

43. *Symbol* has here a specific sense, completely different from that of *mythical* conscience of the symbol in E. Cassirer, *Philosophie der symbolischen Formen*, Bruno Cassirer, Berlin 1923 (transl.: *The philosophy of symbolic forms*, Yale University Press, New Haven/ London 1953).

such dynamic quality) but also—without objectifying the perceived or framed nature—to the conceptual thought. Its ontological status has, in other words, aesthetic value. The word *aesthesis*, "visual perception", implies the primacy of sight. It is through the aesthetic vision that the subject regains nature, appropriating it through representations. The aesthetic experience refers, at least according to Kant's *Critique of Judgement*, to a specific order, non-narrative, which breaks with daily life. It transcends every logical determination and momentarily blends the subject and its object. It *con-fuses* and unites him through or in the encounter with an object: a work of art, at first; nature, after.

Nature can be aesthetically experienced after having desired to get it back, or better, get back the relationship with it. A motivated relationship, induced by the subject who shows interest in nature. However, when it happens, it happens disinterestedly, *surprising* the subject. The aesthetic experience of nature is at the same time the result of mediation (thus intentional) and of immediacy (it happens in a single moment). It combines the wait and the unexpected, the interest and the lack of it, and is both subjective and general. It goes beyond the subject-nature boundary, which is at the basis of the search for nature, and confuses the two poles within the phenomenon. Such relationship with nature, even if intimately sought after for, takes, in the aesthetic experience, the form of an encounter, an event[44]. The relationship with nature, the driving force and goal of the subject's search is, in a strict sense, invisible and impossible to represent. The image, tangible and real, gets there anyway, serving at the same time as source of aesthetic pleasure. The desire to recreate the relationship with nature is intellectual and moral but the re-appropriation, the regained relationship, absolutely is not: it is purely aesthetic. It is not only by going *towards* nature that the subject can find it. Being within nature, inspecting it to its most intimate details, often reinforces the conviction of non-belonging and that of the fundamental difference which separates man from nature. The relationship is created through and within the image and takes, at first, the shape of a landscape-image. The latter does not work as a fusion between subject and nature; rather, it reveals

44. G. Simmel, *Philosophie der Landschaft*, 637.

9 Leonardo da Vinci, *Landscape* (study), 1473, (Galleria degli Uffizi, Florence)

an idea of nature with which the subject could, if necessary, aesthetically blend. As landscape-image, the representation of nature always works—at least in the so-called Western tradition[45] —thanks to the framing. It offers a piece of nature that refers, beyond the visible borders, to an invisible wholeness. The framing mechanism forces the receptive eye to occupy the place starting from which it creates a (mental) representation of the (pictorial) representation. *In front of* the representation of nature the subject already produces *something*; but the fusion between the observer and the observed only concerns the relationship between the subject and a work of art, a human artifact. The following relationship, coming much later, and also designated with the word "landscape", indicates the bond between man and nature. The "thirst for nature" takes form in the seventeenth-century—one need only think of the extraordinary success of landscape in the Netherlands—in image *in primis*, and not in the perception of lived spaces.

45. See H. Maldiney, *Ouvrir le rien. L'art nu*, Encre Marine, La Versanne 2000, 43-44.

To appropriate nature through art means to overlap one representation onto another. The neologism "landscape" precisely expresses the appeal of these particular objects, these paintings of a new genre, which render nature as such and no more as a mere natural setting. Landscapes, painted on urban buildings' walls, bring nature back *to the city*. Technical, aesthetic and philosophic reasons initially cause the image to not "work" completely. "To work" implies to supply a correct visual framework that allows to contain that vision of nature which the spectator, placed in an ideal position, can see and create. The development of different ways of representation is also intimately linked to the city and its way of "seeing" things. The famous experience of Brunelleschi—who, using an optical device, demonstrated the principles of one-point perspective—in the heart of Florence supplied, on the basis of a concrete model, an intellectual and technical *framework* applicable to reality and usable in painting. It is this urban gaze that would later be transposed into art, a gaze that Leonardo da Vinci, in 1473, projects onto nature, thus creating one of the first "free" landscapes.

The history of the landscape-image—that has been synonym of that of landscape genre for a long time but which, on closer inspection, is broader, for it also includes drawing, engraving, etc.—testifies to the various representations of nature across the centuries until the moment of the complete exclusion of the human figure. The landscape *without* human figures of the second half of the eighteenth-century allows the viewer to project himself into the pictorial space in a different way. This happens more or less at the same moment in which the experience of the empirical landscape spreads throughout Europe. The painting, being an intermediate object between nature and subject, leaves then space to the actual fusion of the two poles of the relationship; such fusion will, in turn, influence the art of landscape.

CHAPTER IV

LANDSCAPE AND TIME

The deeply historical dimension of landscape—its initial development, its rise within the history of art, of literature and gardens, its becoming represented landscape and lived landscape, raises a series of questions. Firstly, it implies a distinction between ages of landscape and non-landscape ages and, of no lesser importance, the exclusion—on both a temporal and a global level—of non-landscape cultures and civilizations. Such an approach, even if supported by historical evidence, appears to be immediately problematic because of its basic postulate, which considers the existence of fundamentally different *worlds* within humanity. Why, then, only analyze landscape ages of landscape cultures and not question the subject, necessarily general and abstract, of these entities in general? Would it not be better to always consider *a* single subject, an individual with his particular history, aware of the difficulties, of course, in formulating a theory based on what, by definition, escapes generalizations? Or should we rather think of the subject of landscape in terms of a collective subjectivity? The answer has to be sought in the facts—which can be controlled and interpreted—through documents and historical traces. It are the facts facts allow, or demand, periodization and inclusion-exclusion logic.

Available informations lead us to date the appearance of landscape in the third-century B.C. The idyll, a highly artificial poetic genre created by Theocritus, is a tangible proof of that. In his poems, tributary to the urban culture—which we associate to the first well documented metropolis of ancient times, Alexandria—nature is definitely *on the outside*, that is outside the field of action of everyday life. In Theocritus's vision, the countryside is already the object of a nostalgic longing. He appeals to the poet-citizen-pseudo-shepherd, who projects on nature the ideals of a simple life. The shepherd, the man who, in the perspective of the urban gaze—by now alienated and far from nature—never lost the relation with it, is the voice through which the recovery of nature takes place. In the idylls, the countryside takes the form of a nature closer to earthly paradise, completely different from the earlier evocations of the classical period, always rational and objective:

> But Eucrite and I and pretty Amyrituas
> Turned towards Phasidamos' farm, there we lay down rejoicing
> On deep beds of sweet-smelling rushes and freshly stripped vine leaves.

10 Jürg Kreienbühl, *The Shelter* (*L'abri en carton*), 1970

> Overhead rustled many black poplars and elm trees,
> And Sacred water chuckled and gurgled nearby
> As it trickled forth from the caves of the nymphs.
> Dusky locusts were hard at their chirping on shady branches,
> And from afar the tree frog crooned in a dense thorn bush,
> And the crested larks and the linnet sang, and the turtle dove mooned,
> And the yellow bees buzzed as they hovered around the clear spring.
> All was fragrant with rich summer, the odours of fruit time.
> Pears lay by our feet, by our sides apples
> In lavish abundance were rolling, and the boughs
> Of the plum trees, heavy laden drooped to the ground.[1]

It is the poet and the refined citizen's subjectivity that shines through these verses, formulated with irony and precision. Hence, the personification of nature, the projection of feelings onto it. In the bucolic genre everything is image, fiction: the shepherd wears the mask of the poet, while nature serves as a simulacrum of the ideal, which the poet transposes onto it. We, readers of Theocritus, get in touch with nature through art (the nature described by the poet belongs to the aesthetic sphere), in an impossible, oxymoronic enunciation, the idyll being artifice and, at the same time, extreme simplicity. It has to be said that we ignore almost everything about the iconic representations of nature of the Hellenistic period. The poetic representation invented by Theocritus shows, however, the development of a literary scene built with the *summum* of the most sophisticated art, within which nature is always seen as image. If the history of art will later know landscape-images in the form of a "window" that opens onto imaginary spaces, the author of the Idylls seems to already be offering a series of "literary windows" that allow, through poetic discourse, the creation of an *image of nature*.

Theocritus thus presented a literary landscape, something Classical Greek literature never did. Considering classical literature in general, it appears that its relationship with nature only very rarely represents a fact of primary importance. The descriptions and evocations of nature, in epic, dramatic or lyrical works, short or long, general or specific, have always had a subordinate function.

1. *The Idylls of Theocritus*, transl.:
T. Sargent, W. W. Norton, New York 1986.

11 Roman fresco with a mythological landscape, Museo Archeologico Nazionale di Napoli

The focus of the attention revolves exclusively around the human being, and nature matters only in relation to man. Experience and observation, decisive in the Greek context, do not allow to cross the threshold of the aesthetic sphere of landscape; rather, it concerns just the practical and ethical dimension of the country[2]. Even when, unusually, the beauty of a region is evoked, the specific, analytic and economic gaze on useful realities imposes itself. Regarding the description of natural scenes, the Greek man is, like Schiller already noticed: "to the highest degree precise, faithful and circumstantial in describing them, yet simply no more so and with no more preferential involvement of his heart than he displays in the description of a tunic, a shield or a suit of armour, some domestic article, or any mechanical product".[3]

2. For the famous cave of Calypso and landscape (*The Odyssey*) see M. Jakob, *Paesaggio e letteratura*, Olschki, Florence 2005, 5.
3. F. Schiller, *Über naive und sentimentalische Dichtung* (transl.: *On Naïve and Sentimental Poetry*, in *German Aesthetic and Literary Criticism: Winckelmann, Lessing, Hamann, Herder, Schiller and Goethe*, ed. H. B. Nesbit, Cambridge University Press, Cambridge 1985, 189).

In the Roman age we can identify a second stage of the proto-history of landscape. The innovation takes place mainly in the field of painting, even if it "illustrates", in most cases, literary motifs. The mural paintings of Roman villas display nature in minute detail, as well as through heroic impressions derived from Homeric adventures or bucolic scenes. These are images that clearly allow to "watch through" the wall, projecting the viewer in fantastic, grotesque, idyllic or playful spaces. The framing of theseoften very explicit landscapes underscores the artifice of the internal image, which opens on a fascinating "outside". Moreover, these works represent an example of *semiosis* (Jakobson) of great complexity. They translate literature into images and, at the same time, have an architectural function, which is extended on the outside of the walls through the art of gardens. We ignore almost everything about the origins and codes of these ancient landscapes: do they come from Greece? Are they of Hellenistic origin? Or, rather, are they a specifically Roman invention?[4] Their great popularity, especially in the Augustan age, is however undeniable. Vitruvius refers to them in a famous passage of his *De Architectura*:

> For by painting an image is made of what is, or of what may be; for example, men, buildings, ships, and other objects; of these definite and circumscribed bodies, imitations are taken and fashioned in their likeness. Hence the ancients who first used polished stucco, began by imitating the variety and arrangement of marble inlay; then the varied distribution of festoons, ferns, coloured strips. Then they proceeded to imitate the contours of buildings, the outstanding projections of columns and gables; in open spaces, like exedrae, they designed scenery on a large scale in tragic, comic, or satyric style; in covered promenades, because of the length of the walls, they used for ornament the varieties of landscape gardening, finding subjects in the characteristics of particular places; for they paint harbours, headlands, shores, rivers, springs, straits, temples, groves, hills, cattle, shepherds.[5]

4. See R. Ling, *Roman Painting*, Cambridge University Press, Cambridge 1991, 142; cf. H. Mielsch, *Römische Wandmalerei*, WBG, Darmstadt 2001.

5. Marco Vitruvio Pollione, *De architectura*, Studio Tesi, Rome 1993, 329 (VII, 5); transl.: *On Architecture*, Harvard University Press, London 1934.

The Roman theorist confirms the use of perspective and the tight bond between landscape and architecture, the interiors of buildings. He also underscores the connection with scenic design and already deplores the grotesque and illusory excesses of his times: "But these which were imitations based upon reality are now disdained by the improper taste of the present. On the stucco are monsters rather than definite representations taken from definite things."[6] In an equally famous note of the *Naturalis Historia*, Pliny the Elder identified the inventor of the genre (Latin does not have a word for "landscape", hence the use of the term *topiaria opera*) with a certain Ludius or Studius, who depicted

> [...] villas, porticos, ornamental gardening, woods, groves, hills, fishponds, canals, rivers, sea-shores, and anything else one could desire; varied with figures of persons walking, sailing, or proceeding to their villas, on asses or in carriages. Then, too, there are others to be seen fishing, fowling, or gathering in the vintage[7].

The third decisive age, which extends to the present day, debuts at the end of the Middle Ages. Starting from the fourteenth-century it coincides with the rise of the urban culture, the mercantile society and the appropriation of space. The history of the landscape genre in European painting is the sensitive trace and the cultural cornerstone of a fundamental development. In fact, through proto-landscapes and landscapes of this tradition, it is possible to read the different ways of representing nature and deduce their major implications. The only constant—and this until the revolution started by Claude Monet in the second half of the nineteenth-century—is the fact that such representations, whether they are of a religious, mythological, political order, or something else entirely, all work on the basis of a *vis-à-vis* approach, with nature visible *in front of* the spectator.

---

6. *Ibidem.*
7. Pliny the Elder, **The Natural History,** transl.: J. Bostock, H. T. Riley, H. G. Bohn, London 1857, XXXV, 116.

The landscape genre and the representation

The famous fresco of *Palazzo Pubblico* in Siena, painted by Ambrogio Lorenzetti and known as *The Allegory of Good and Bad Government* (Ill. 8), gives, for the first time in post-antique Western art, a perception of nature worked by man, starting from a principally urban point of view [8]. Within it we can identify the clear separation between the city—proud of itself—and the countryside, but also the symbiosis of the two, symbolized by trade at the "border". Nature, here, is used, domesticated; it is a dominion that derives from the city and materializes in the image of the citizen-knight who flies over the scene, like the spectator to whom this representation of parts of territory is offered. Representing the country, the place subjected to the control of the city—situated on a higher ground—means to appropriate it, to transcribe it on an image (the image, but also the gaze, the very fact of looking, in fact belongs to the city) that goes beyond cartography to open, spatially, in the direction of the future landscape. Here, nature is not yet represented or searched as such, but only as (political) territory or (agricultural, economic) country. It is occupied, formed, and deformed (the *locus terribilis* of the lacerated territory) by the man who, aware of his deeds and misdeeds does not refer to a fascination with nature, but rather to its control. The aesthetical aspect concerns mainly the urban dominion, which is self-represented in the arabesque of the dance or in the sensual beauty of the costumes.

The external dominion in itself remains non-aesthetical, the territory of an "outside" that only the gaze of the city is able to ennoble.

About a century later we find once again, in the *Madonna of Chancellor Rolin* by Jan van Eyck, the same sinuous river with its graceful bridge next to the territorial division of urban areas, agricultural or not. While the gaze on nature was not the main theme of Lorenzetti's fresco (no horizon in front of us), van Eyck makes it one of the relevant objects of his work. The painting appears to be the place where two opposing positions face each other: the first one, dictated by theology and personified by the figure of the Chancellor, a powerful man of the Church, indicates the absolute primacy (the

---

8. See J. Wamberg, *Abandoning Paradise: The Western Pictorial Paradigm Shift around 1420,* in *Technologies of Landscape: From Reaping to Recycling,* ed. D. Nye, University of Massachusetts Press, Amherst 2000, 69-86.

12 Jan van Eyck, *The Madonna of Chancellor Rolin*, 1435, (Louvre, Paris)

13 detail, Jan van Eyck, *The Madonna of Chancellor Rolin*, 1435 (Louvre, Paris)

foreground) of religion. It is based—inside a palace, a closed system—on the internal vision that relies on the Holy Scriptures; the second position hinges on a gaze, both exposed and bare, and leaves the sacred to "get lost" in the world, in the "naturally" unlimited space. It is symbolized by two figures who perceive, from an elevated point of view, an extremely rich and detailed reality. The gaze encompasses both the domesticated world of the city and countryside and the mountain range against the distant horizon.

Here, too, the city allows for the perception of nature. The two figures—one facing backwards, the other one watching it—are "observers"; they do not belong to the dominant religious construction, but are part of the interstitial space between the sacred and the world, the *hortus conclusus* represented by the garden-balcony. On the one hand, their relative smallness symbolizes the act of getting lost, of descending into the world. On the other hand, though, the two can resist the dizzying height, measuring the spatial depth. It is their gaze, before the spectacle of nature, in front of the epiphany of the bright open space, which van Eyck's pictorial reflection ostentatiously displays. It is a space of freedom—freedom of movement, life,

14 Joachim Patinir, *The Rest on the Flight into Egypt*, 1515-1525 (Gemäldegalerie, Berlin)

trade—much different from the closed and protective one of faith; hence the relation between self-sufficient, isolated space and eternal time on one side, and open space and human time, as far as the eye can see, on the other. An antinomy split through the meaningful relationship of the Chancellor with the Heavenly city of Jerusalem on the right, and the terrestrial realm—in the direction of the figure with the red turban (the painter himself?)—on the left.

The visual relationship with nature as the object of naïve desire (which does not understand the unreality of the sensitive things of this world), but also as a compelling attraction (it diagonally transcends the sacred interior of the Church, passes through the house of God, drawing to itself the gaze of the spectator) is, in today's perspective, the essential element of this painting. What van Eyck displayed thus seems to be an early *mise en abyme* of the representation of nature, namely of the landscape-image as an object of desire. Using the point of view occupied by the two figures as a theatrical device—it is in this scene, adorned with allegorical symbols such as the three peacocks, two magpies, five flowers, that the two figures succumb to the contemplation of the world—, van Eyck illustrates the temptation of the visual relationship with nature as such. The landscape, framed and marked out by solemn arcades and filtered by the gaze of the observers, who are, at the same time, delegates of the spectator, anticipates through its unlikely stretch (linking the infinitely small to the infinitely big) the *Weltlandschaften*, the world-landscapes of Joachim Patinir. The religious absolute, the holy infinite, translated by Patinir into an earthly infinite, slips towards an outside world that culminates in the horizon, namely towards an invisible line that connects the earth (the mountains) to the sky, a line which is essential for the visual construction of the whole thing but, also, on the horizontal level, for the relationship between the Chancellor and the Virgin.

From the second half of the fifteenth-century it is possible to encounter another way of representing and approaching nature. Leonardo, Dürer and Altdorfer practice in nature, outdoors. Their respective works, probably realized during excursions or travels[9], are marginal and "invisible" according to the rhetorical-aesthetical standards of the times (and even according to the norms of painting that, until the nineteenth-century, favor narration and grand style, consequently reducing the landscape to a function of background). These unusual images of nature—Leonardo, in his *Treatise on Painting*, asserted: "What induces you, O man, to depart from your home in town, to leave parents and friends, and go to the countryside over mountains and valleys, if it is not the beauty of the world of nature which, if you consider well, you can only enjoy through the sense of sight?"[10] —are, in most cases, without a protagonist. They present both inhabited territories, a nature domesticated by man, and almost wild spots. What is surprising about these small-scale works which look like notes, is the subjectivity of the result. The speed of the stroke, the materials employed, the liberty that the artist—not subjected to standardized artistic criteria—takes once he leaves the workshop, all of this leads to representations that, despite their great precision and veracity, bear witness, through the aesthetic gaze on nature, to a personal style. It is as if a the real encounter has tak-

---

9. See, for Dürer, his return from Italy to Germany in 1495.
10. Leonardo da Vinci, *Trattato della pittura* (transl.: *The Notebooks of Leonardo da Vinci*, ed.: T. Wells, Oxford University Press, New York 2008, 206).

en place between a subject, or better, an individuality, and nature, materialized in the form of minute landscapes. These sketches or studies will, however, be considered pictorial landscapes only much later, in light of the *lived* experience of landscape that spreads from the eighteenth-century. These works are at the same time too small (they cannot be exhibited as a canvas, inviting the spectator to identify himself with the respective landscape; they remain intimist and belong, so to speak, to the experimental sphere of their authors), too exceptional and too marginal to be part of the landscape genre, considered, for a long time, as minor and relegated to the category of the *parerga*.[11] They represent, actually, the earliest prototypes of the encounter between art and the landscape experience[12].

The genre demands the necessary presence of one or more human figures in the landscape, namely its employment "as a servant to their other peeces, to illustrate or sett of their Historicall painting by filling up the empty Corners, or void places of Figures and story, with some fragment of Lanscape"[13]. In Patinir, in Giorgione—whose famous *Tempest* has been the first work to be identified as "land"

---

11. See H. Peacham, *The Art of Drawing with the Pen,* London 1606, 28: "Seldome is it drawne by it selfe, but in respect and for the sake of something else: wherefore it falleth among those things which we call *Parerga*".
12. This work is situated **outside** of the sphere of painting; it is part of Leonardo's philosophical research on nature, in painting it is possible to invent landscapes: "*How to increase your talent and stimulate various inventions*. Look at walls splashed with a number of stains, or stones of various mixed colours. If you have to invent some scene, you can see the resemblances to a number of landscapes, adorned with mountains, rivers, rocks, trees, great plains, valleys and hills, in various ways. Also you can see various battles, and lively postures of strange figures, expressions on faces, costumes and an infinite number of things, which you can reduce to good integrated form. This happens on such walls and varicoloured stones, (which act) like the sound of bells, in whose pealing you can find every name and word that you can imagine. Do not despise my opinion, when I remind you that it should not be hard for you to stop sometimes and look into the stains of walls, or ashes of a fire, or clouds, or mud or like places, in which, if you consider them well, you may find really marvellous ideas. The mind of the painter is stimulated to new discoveries, the composition of battles of animals and men, various compositions of landscapes and monstrous things, such as devils and similar things, which may bring you honour, because by indistinct things the mind is stimulated to new inventions." (Leonardo da Vinci, *Trattato della pittura*, 173-174)
13. E. Norgate, *Miniatura or the Art of Limning*, ed.: M. Hardie, Oxford University Press, Oxford 1919, 49.

(paese) in the modern sense of landscape[14] —in Titian and countless other painters of the fifteenth-, sixteenth- and seventeenth-century, the landscape-image usually works with the support of figures who face us, viewers of the painting. The human figure occupies, in other words, the space imagined by van Eyck, but it turns around, so to speak, to look us in the eye. From now on, the logic of artistic representation changes radically. We now see someone *in* the landscape, a figure starting from which what surrounds it, the landscape, acquires meaning. The figure is usually identifiable; it is part of a religious, mythological or political narrative. "To enter" a landscape means to pass through the history of the figure, in the broad sense of the term. Our gaze on nature implies thus always an indirect approach via the perspective of a person in the painting, who «opens our eyes». This explains the deep theatricality[15] of the genre: the painting is seen as a scene in which the meaning of the background, so important, reveals itself through the messages sent by the figures. The rudimentary spatiality of Lorenzetti's fresco did not allow such identification yet. It did not have central characters (in the sense of the application of the rules of perspective and in a narrative sense) and required a symbolic or cartographic reading: it was necessary to jump from a place, from a represented region to another, to finally reach, following the allegoric message, the idea of totality. Instead, the van Eyck of *Chancellor Rolin* imposes a predestined point of view, but only to better deconstruct it, giving it the immature and mysterious identity linked to the two characters, "incomplete", who succumb to the appearance of the sensitive world. Dürer and Altdorfer's watercolors do not have a point of view represented inside the image itself and thus present us with the problem of the distance necessary to "enter" these works (it is, after all, the historical distance that allowed us to recognize them). Young Leonardo da Vinci's drawing shows, instead of a point of view

---

14. "The small landscape with the storm, the gipsy woman and the soldier executed by the hand of Zorzi da Castelfranco" (*Anonimo Morelliano*, ed.: T. Frommel, Graeser, Vienna 1888, 106).
15. See E. Turri, *Il paesaggio come teatro. Dal territorio vissuto al territorio rappresentato,* Marsilio, Venice 2003; S. Daniels, D. Cosgrove, **Spectacle and Text: Landscape Metaphors in Cultural Geography**, in *Place/Culture/Representation*, ed.: J. Duncan, D. Ley, Routledge, London 1993, 57-77.

15 Claude Lorrain, *Landscape with the Rest on the Flight into Egypt* (*Noon*), 1666, Hermitage, St. Petersburg

expressed through a figure, the application of perspective in action. It is as if the artist layered the *veil* or the *reticulated net*—that is the visual pattern of the perspective representation—on the country in front of him. This drives us to identify as a founding point of view the technological device itself, masterly handled by the painter.

Claude Lorrain, probably the most influential "landscape painter" of all time, embodies both the apogee and the transformation of the model based on the human figure. With the great French painter who, according to his own words, sold the landscape and offered the figures for free (sometimes painted by other artists, such as Filippo Lunari), the theatricality of the genre reaches the paroxysm. Everything, in Lorrain, is the result of a thorough composition, a pictorial discourse that arranges the elements with the purpose of obtaining a more intense effect on the spectator. Art, in Lorrain, is the expression of a rhetoric, which confines to his landscapes the character of an assembly of *loci*.

16 Claude Lorrain, *Coastal Landscape with Apollo and the Cumean Sibyl*, Hermitage, St. Petersburg

Lorrain's nature—identified by some as the "ideal landscape"—is completely fake, the result of total composition, a skillful mixture of various elements for a bursting effect of the created image. The artist transforms his observations and invents an Italy, which is neither truly ancient, nor truly contemporary, an imaginary country on the pursuit of the golden age. He proposes a vision of a peaceful nature, close to divine and human figures, in other words a world that is totally unlikely. Or rather, in Goethe's words, his "pictures have the highest truth but no trace of actuality"[16]. The truth of nature resides then in the technique of the painter; in the manner he renders light, shade and depth. Lorrain provides, in other words, a vision of non-existent places, and he does so according to the rules of classical rhetoric and spatial overlapping of the first, second and third levels,

16. J.P. Eckermann, *Gespräche mit Goethe in den letzten Jahren seines Lebens*, Insel, Frankfurt am Main 2006 (transl.: *Conversations of Goethe with Johann Peter Eckermann*, Da Capo Press, Boston 1998).

described in Gian Paolo Lomazzo's *Trattato dell'arte della pittura* (1584): "Because the lands have to be shown in three different parts. The first has to be visible from a close range. The second, more dazzled, and the third has to vanish, almost, fade into infinite"[17]. The effect of summary achieved by Lorrain—the fact that the painting exists only as an analytical sum of distinct elements, as it actually is—is mainly due to his technique. The latter is so persuasive that it makes us forget about the work of composition, to the advantage of the magic of the whole thing. The impressive pictorial "development" realized by the artist also causes, however, the sensitive modification of the role reserved to the figures in the image. With Lorrain, the protagonists get lost in the landscape and become secondary; they are merely decorative, while the landscape, once only a simple background, becomes substantial and hence expands its dominion.

This new form of representation defines at the same time a "true" space; the spectator can indeed project himself into it "naturally", without passing through the intermediation of the figures that carry him in "their" space. Lorrain, therefore, partially blurs the access codes of landscape representation. The figures are no longer the main support for "entering" the painted space: perception now proceeds directly and the window-scene opens by itself, or, better, supports itself, ironically, thanks to other components such as ruins or trees, true protagonists of the canvases of the master. The tree, the heroic *pars pro toto* of nature, is the omnipresent symbol of the victory of Nature over the human (narrative) factor.[18] The straightness and verticality of the tree take the place of the potentially anachronistic figures.

The ruins, the constructions of human origin recovered from nature[19], are an additional sign of such dethronement. It seems im-

17. G.P. Lomazzo, *Trattato dell'arte della pittura, scoltura, et architettura,* Milan 1584, 473 (transl.: *A tracte containing the artes of curious paintinge, carvinge, and building,* Oxford 1598, reprint Gregg International, London 1970).
18. See G.B. Aguzzi, *Impresa per dipingere l'historia d'Erminia,* quoted in Busch, *Landschaftsmalerei,* Reimer, Berlin 1997, vol. III, 106: "And to make the landscape appear more natural, if possible, it would be good to include some palms and plane trees, sycamores, mastic trees, and some other more typical of our lands, olive trees, laurels, elms, oaks, ashes and apple trees and figs".
19. G. Simmel, *Die Ruine,* in *Philosophische Kultur. Gesammelte Essays,* Insel, Leipzig 1911 (transl.: *The Ruin* in *Georg Simmel 1858-1918,* Ohio State University Press, Columbus 1959).

portant, given Lorrain's fundamental role in the history of art, but also in the history of ideas and of landscape architecture, to point out the peculiarity of his paintings. As an artist who evaluates and controls the effect of painting according to the rules of rhetoric, he is as distant as possible from a "strong feeling in front of nature", later claimed by the likes of Constable or Cézanne. In Lorrain, nature is an invention, the result of a long and complicated assembly realized in his studio. The spatiality, achieved through technical means, and the weakening or negation of the human figure—the scenic platform, traditionally the place of the revelation of the overall meaning, serves here to dethrone the characters, to make them disappear, it works as a "storage" of obsolete figures—they seem to announce the triumph of nature. This nature, apparently the true target of the paintings, is however always an inhabited nature; we encounter always cultural landscapes, that is pieces of land marked for a long time by the presence of man. The triumphing nature still refers to the human being and his impact on the "land", but it does so under the sign of the *past*.

The temporal aspect is decisive for the understanding of Lorrain's (and other painters') works, as well as for that of landscape in general[20]. Usually, we easily associate landscape and space, forgetting the second and fundamental category: time. According to the definition of the geographer Yi Fu Tuan, landscape is, instead, precisely the irruption of time in space: "Every perspective landscape painting or photograph teaches us to see time 'flowing' through space"[21].

The artistic representations of landscape that we discussed up to here all reveal a complex temporal dimension. Lorenzetti's fresco illustrates an exemplar, typical time: that, regular and organized, of the farmers' or citizens' life and that, equally regulated, of trade; but also that, unique, of celebrations. The proto-landscape scene of the Palazzo Pubblico of Siena does not fix a moment, rather it refers to a general time: the farmers seed, work, and harvest at the same time. Van Eyck's *Madonna of Chancellor Rolin* distinguishes the infinite time of religious meditation and the real presence of the holy figures from the temporality of worldly life. The latter, symbolized

---

20. See M. Jakob, *Paysage et temps*, Infolio, Gollion 2007.

21. Yi Fu Tuan, *Space and Place: The Perspective of Experience*, Arnold, London 1977, 124.

firstly by the river, the time that relentlessly slips away, is one of the human activities that has shaped the territory. The freeze-frame, the temporary fusion of space and time, refers demonstratively to the perspective of the observers; with them we live *one* instant of the world that has become image, while the exemplary believer, the Chancellor, seems to belong to the eternal realm of the holy duration, that is eternity.

Figures that are normally arranged in front of us in landscapes allow our transference into "their" space, as well as our participation in "their" time. Whether it is the Virgin Mary fleeing to Egypt or a melancholic Venus or a Saint George during the fight, it is always their being there in that precise moment that gives meaning to the surrounding nature. The temporal layers of the composition, present in most landscapes, are explained by the depicted character. The heading *landscape* in Diderot and d'Alembert's *Encyclopédie* states this very clearly:

> Sometimes we represent uncultivated and uninhabited sites in landscape painting so as to have the liberty to paint the bizarre effects of nature's livery, and the jumbled and irregular formations of undeveloped land. But this sort of imitation could not move us other than in moments of melancholy, where the thing imitated in the picture sympathized with our passions. In any other state, the most beautiful landscape painting , were it by Titian or Carracci, would not interest us more than the view of a canton of a frightful or pleasant country. There is nothing in such a picture that speaks to us, one might say, and as it barely touches us, it does not engage us very much. Intelligent painters have rightly sensed this truth so they rarely made landscape paintings deserted and without figures[22].

Now, as we've emphasized, in Lorrain the figures do not assume any more this role of guide or conscience through which the spectator can project himself into the landscape. On the one hand, he does not need to, since the space he is interested in opens without "external" help (Nature, in the 17th century, is considered

---

22. This definition of *landscape* is the English translation supplied by *The Encyclopedia of Diderot & d'Alembert, collaborative translation project*, available at http://quod.lib.umich.edu/d/did.

interesting as such). On the other hand, the structural weakness of the characters (their identity is mostly decorative, and we can easily imagine to interchange figures from one painting to another[23]) enhances the landscape, forcing the viewer himself to question a representation no more fully explained by historic elements or by the extra-pictorial sense. By weakening the role of the human figure, the painter adds to the ease of situating oneself within the painting, he sharpens the attention and stimulates a more demanding form of reception. It is now equally the task of the spectator to provide a sense to the representation of nature on the basis of what it includes. The receptive action becomes therefore more complex, and, above all, it turns into an aesthetic experience with its own temporality.

Therefore, it is not a coincidence if in Lorrain's landscapes we find so many temporal markers: the undefined time of figures lost in their static world (mythological, biblical characters, etc.); the human time of everyday characters (shepherds, people working in the fields); the cyclical time of nature; the effect of time on manmade constructions (ruins of all sort). The most important temporal layer, in Lorrain's paintings, is however the past: the absolute past of the idealized characters; the historical past of the artifacts; the melancholic past of ruins; but also Nature itself as a "world" that gets older once we can glimpse the end of the golden age. The energy of nature, in itself potentially hostile to man, is tamed in the topical image of old, solitary trees.

The subtle changes in Lorrain's works imply, however, a higher awareness towards nature. In the same historical period in which his Northern colleagues interpret nature as a reality significant in and for itself, he identifies lived or domesticated nature as already provided with a meaning. He encourages us to read the signs scattered around in nature, paths, trails, bridges, creeks, ponds, rivers, hills, trees, giving them a meaning *a priori*. In Lorrain's vision nature has, as much as humans, a past and a history and thus it will no longer be scary, while the wild nature still made the seventeenth-century man shiver. The idealized image of a nature tamed and at peace thus contributed to its further domestication.

---

23. See F.T. Vischer, *Sentimentalität und Staffage*, in O. Bätschmann, *Entfernung der Natur. Landschaftsmalerei 1750-1920*, Dumont, Cologne 1989, 314-317.

In the Netherlands, a strong demand for paintings representing landscapes will determine in the seventeenth-century the specialization of a great number of painters well-versed in these motifs. In the heart of a century characterized by scientific observation and the will to describe the world precisely through cartographic and pictorial transcription of reality, painting will be based chiefly on the optical model, that is on what happens in the eye, leaving aside the classical "Italian" model of perspectival construction.

The significant and varied presence of nature is however linked to a formidable transformation, which invested at that time the whole region. The northern part of the Netherlands earned, in fact, a substantial part of a new territory retrieved from the sea, managing the obtained areas in a strictly geometrical way. The territorial identity built over the centuries resulted completely shaken: the new lands added to the existing ones, grown organically until that moment, highlighted the extreme contrast between old and new.

The territorial crisis, that is the separation between the grown and the built land, together with the radical crisis of perception due to two among the centuries biggest inventions, the telescope and the microscope, had a direct impact on the methods of representation and on the objects shown in contemporary landscape painting. Another essential factor, besides the doubts raised by optical theory and philosophy, is the theology of the time, the feeling of detachment and a new way to look at nature preached by Protestantism. All these factors brought about a form of landscape painting marked by the disappearance of narrative intentions and sometimes even that of the human figure itself, to the advantage of a natural setting seen as an intelligible, or intelligent reality (Spinoza). The abandonment of the narrative element definitively freed the gaze and pointed to an increasingly autonomous cultural landscape. In the Netherlands the anthropic landscape does not refer anymore to extraordinary human adventures (religious, mythological); it rather "speaks" of the old disappearing country (see the countless windmills, farms and ferryboats), of the wealth of a nation (the famous Dutch cows as political symbols) or of everyday human activities (like fishing).

The narration, the supply of a founding pre-text, disappears sometimes completely, leaving space to an overwhelming void, where the huge sky or the enormous stretch of perceived land, unreadable by humans, reduce man to almost nothing. It is in this reduced and almost invisible form that we encounter the solitary figure, lost in a sublime scenery, which escapes human control. In such a context, the desire for nature, for its aestheticization and its possession through a powerful image (the painting), privileges two principal aspects or types: the representation of the past and the melancholic sublime.

The first possibility regards the action of time and the natural forces that have created in the past a familiar country. Church towers, turrets, windmills, chimney stacks and fishermen's boats, in short a whole artistic repertoire later labelled with the term "picturesque", gives the sense of a continuity, an organic development and a tradition within a protecting nature. The second case, sublime landscape *ante litteram*, presents a series of scenes out of scale from which man has been deposed, faced as he is with the unlimited and incomparably great power of nature. Lorrain's tree (Nature personified) is here overturned, fallen, and becomes an image of man's decline.

This double triumph of nature transposed inside the houses of the mercantile bourgeoisie is, in spite of the suggested apparent religious humility (man is nothing, nature is everything), however part of a more complex phenomenon. It happens only because the old becomes an aesthetic value thanks to the contrast with the new. The sublime and picturesque beauty of the "old country" results, dialectically, from the ongoing transformation of the territory: it is related to inventions, improvements, and retrievals.

The appeal of the "sublime" landscape is also based on historic premises. The development of the sublime is coupled, as Hartmut Böhme [24] has highlighted, to the continuous effort with which the European bourgeoisie, the dominant class, tried to hoard the last corners of unexplored nature. Landscape has, from this point of view, a different status from that presented by contemporary cartography. Cartography transcribes and claims the control and dominion of the world. It implies the existence of a rational space that cancels the opposition between domesticated and primeval nature: on paper

24. See H. Böhme, *Das Steinerne. Anmerkungen zur Theorie des Erhabenen aus dem Blick des "Menschenfreindesten"*, in *Das Erhabene*, ed.: C. Preis, VCH, Weinheim 1989, 120-141.

17 Caspar David Friedrich, *Woman before the Rising Sun*, 1818-1820 (Folkwang Museum, Essen)

everything is equivalent. On the contrary, one of the main themes of the landscape of the time is the lack of control illustrated by situations in which dominance is transformed into submission or defeat. The human figures are lost in the immensity of nature, abandoned on unsteady or dangerous paths, they are in the middle of a forest or of the sea and often placed in the lower part of the painting, as if they had to bear the weight of an oppressive sky on their shoulders.

At a historical moment when man tries to tame and possess the whole nature, he is, paradoxically, shown as deposed, threatened. Does he already fear, as the Romantics[25] suggested a little later, the "revenge" of nature? Does he fear the disenchantment in front of an unveiled nature, or better, is he concerned by its inevitable destruction? Does he see the vanity of his own action? Or does he face, in the popular sublime visions, a deity (elusive to the human being) consubstantial with the infinite nature? Landscape, the image

---

25. See Böhme, *Das Steinerne*; Id., *Goethes Erde zwischen Natur und Geschichte Erfahrungen von Zeit in der Italienischen Reise*, in «Goethe-Jahrbuch», 1993, 110, 209-227.

through which man perceives, more than through any other medium, nature, becomes, in the landscape painting of the 18th and 19th century, the place where the relationship between man and nature—an actual relationship, lived in a process of exploration—is expressed with persistence.

Caspar David Friedrich reaches a further stage in the representation of nature with his works mainly composed of landscapes. Friedrich is a painter of strong contradictions: he rejects the use of sketches, in order to keep the totality of his works unchanged; yet, he presents repeatedly scenes where the theatrical arrangement and the effect of composition reaches almost a grotesque limit. He expresses a new approach to nature, centered in the experience of landscape, but he does so by using a symbolic-religious and rather anachronistic language. Friedrich's work can be divided into two different parts: the first and most substantial one is characterized by the presence of human figures, alone or in groups, almost always seen from behind. In the second part, after having pushed this solitary figure into the most extreme sites (abysses, mountaintops, hidden places) and "sentencing it to death", he completely eliminates it. From now own, he shows—and this happens in such a radical way for the first time in the history of landscape, besides rare cases such as Hercules Seghers or Thomas Jones—nothing but nature.

The figure seen from behind (*Rückenfigur*), typical of Friedrich, reinforced by its spatial isolation, expresses an essential fact: that the person we discover in these situations is himself characterized by his being related to nature. The viewer in front of a Friedrich painting thus perceives not just a person in front of nature, but rather someone for whom the surrounding nature is essential. The *someone* of Friedrich's landscapes is not a simple traveler who is identifying or admiring a site (quite a recurring theme already in the seventeenth-century). He is clearly not in an instrumental relation with nature; he seems to be immersed in its contemplation. Dutch Golden Age Painting, essential for Friedrich for many reasons, often showed figures separated from nature. These works underscored the immense distance between man, reduced to a tiny dot, and nature, almighty and majestic. Friedrich, however, broadens this distance to the extreme. In his works, the human being—no longer a mere figure but a subjectivity with all its complexity—is radically separated from nature

18 Caspar David Friedrich, *The Monk by the Sea*, 1809 (Alte Nationalgalerie, Berlin)

in front of him, a nature that, for this very reason, he desires more and more fervently. The silent and solitary situations illustrated by the painter express—based on the experience of landscape—a hidden existential drama, man's final and absolute ambition. When exposed to one of Friedrich's works, the spectator discovers a representation of a piece of nature, a piece of nature which, in turn, someone *inside* the painting is trying to visually appropriate in his turn. Friedrich's main theme is therefore the landscape consciousness in action. It is a radically solipsistic act, also and especially if more protagonists share the scene, and an act with an indefinite temporality.

Entering Friedrich's landscapes implies the will to occupy a place that has already been taken by someone else[26], a place that the viewer, in his turn, would like to contemplate. It is a relationship of identity and, at the same time, of difference, that characterizes the spectator's relation with the *other* spectator of nature *inside* the image. We will never know whether or not two figures in the same situation share or not the same landscape or if they each create, on the contrary, each

26. See J.L. Koerner, *Caspar David Friedrich and the Subject of Landscape,* Yale University Press, New Haven 1990.

one a specific landscape for themselves. In the same way, the spectator will also find himself in doubt, separated from the character on the canvas, as the latter is separated from nature. He will never even know if the suggested encounter with nature—the creation of landscape—through the gaze represented in the painting actually has to be understood as having taken place or if it remains only a desire, never reached. To the irritation, both temporal (since when has this figure stood here, in perfect immobility? for how long?) and existential (Friedrich's characters seem to be posing, directed by an unknown force, while being at the same time they completely absorbed by the surrounding nature) comes therefore the receptive or hermeneutical one. Before definitively freeing the representation of nature from the presence of man, Friedrich radicalizes the classical figure-nature relationship. His painting *The Monk by the Sea* (1810) expresses the vision of a dematerialized and empty nature in a scene where almost everything is absorbed by the fog. The sense of metaphysical void has, however, other consequences as well: given that almost nothing can be identified, we are encouraged to look differently to the painting and to discover its more abstract qualities. The solipsistic appearance of the uncanny monk exposed to the extreme and almost hostile nature complete the sense of desolation. They announce the shock caused by naked nature, a nature without presence and human history. Kleist's famous words, according to whom viewing the painting "in its monotony and boundlessness [...] is as if one's eyelids had been cut away"[27] goes well beyond meteorology and extreme topography, as well as the solitary monk's fate. —They refer especially to the reception of a work which, announcing the emptiness of nature, or better, a nature emptied by man, brutally breaks the codes and the habits of landscape reading. Friedrich's landscapes (we talk about some works of the Twenties and Thirties of the nineteenth-century) free themselves from man, moreover, without touching the rules of representation; actually, there will not be a narration anymore, but there will always be a narrator outside the painting. It was Alexandre Cozens, an artist interested both in the theory and practice of pictorial representation, who stirred the usual representations of nature, and this already in the second half of the eighteenth-century. Cozens, who

27. H. von Kleist, *Empfindungen vor Friedrichs Seelandschaft*, in *Sämtliche Werke*, vol. I /7, Schwabe, Basel 1996, 61.

19 Alexander Cozens, *Landscape*, in *A New Method of Assisting the Invention in Drawing Original Compostions of Landscape*, 1785, plate 8

profited from his Italian *Grand Tour* and who was introduced to *en plein air* painting by Claude-Joseph Vernet, redefines painting and its favorite object, landscape, questioning its double origin, perceptive and productive. According to him, nature—an increasingly valued theme—had never been effectively "conveyed"[28].

Landscape, for Cozens, traditionally produced only very predictable effects. The painting has worked for the centuries as the result of a well-planned composition based on central and aerial perspective, on a series of layers, on the primacy of the foreground, etc. This pattern, present in most of the landscape paintings, emerges clearly in the drawing, that is the form of the lines that structures the

---

28. The poet William Wordsworth, himself an enthusiast of nature ("I am a perfect Enthusiast in my admiration of Nature in all her various forms") will, in 1779, say the same about poetry, "The moment was important in my poetical history; for I date from it my consciousness of the infinite variety of natural appearances which had been unnoticed by the poets of any age or country." (W. Wordsworth, *An Evening Walk*, ed.: J. Averill, Cornell University Press, Ithaca-London 1984, 3).

entire composition. The academic tradition, focused on preparatory drawings, distorts the empirical perception, which does not see lines but, rather, differences in brightness (light-shade) or colors:

> To sketch in the common way, is to transfer ideas from the mind to the paper, on canvas, in outlines, in the slightest manner. To blot, is to make varied spots and shapes with ink on paper, producing accidental forms without lines, from which ideas are presented to the mind. This is conformable to nature: for in nature, forms are not distinguished by lines, but by shade and colour. To sketch, is to delineate ideas; blotting suggests them.[29]

The continued observation of nature on site, the attempts to render it in its "perceived" form[30] and not through a technique applied artificially to it, as well as the criticism of the classical dogma of the primacy of line over color, led Cozens to the development of his *New Method*. It is based on blots, stains on paper thanks to which the artist will be able to "invent" his landscapes (in fact, the title of one of Cozens's essays is: *An Essay to Facilitate the Invention of Landskips*). The concept of invention seems, at first sight, a deviation from reality, which, on the other hand, is explicitly sought after. The disposition of the blots on the paper[31] takes its origin, however, from the interior image that the painter has in his mind even before getting to work (possess your mind strongly with a subject)[32]. During the process of translation, which mixes the subconscious with the conscious, the artist creates an *analogon* of what he has imagined. The artistic production imagined by Cozens prevents, in other words, the projection of preconceived schemes—inevitable, according to the classical method—on the result. As in empirical perception, which does not distinguish spatial layers or lines, but uncovers a totality characterized by bright or chromatic intensities, the invented landscape is able to capture the surface of visual impressions, the (real) one that expresses itself immediately, before any analysis.

---

29. A. Cozens, *A New Method of Assisting the Invention in Drawing Original Compositions of Landscape*, London 1785-86, 2.
30. "This theory is, in fact, the art of seeing properly." (*Ibid.*)
31. "The artificial blot is a production of chance, with a small degree of design." (*Ibid.*)
32. *Ibid.*

20 Monet's *Nymphéas* in the Orangerie, Paris, 1927

Cozens's experimental method had direct repercussions on painters such as Joseph Wright of Derby, William Gilpin, Gainsborough or Constable. Moreover, it anticipates, on the practical and theoretical levels of the representation of nature, Impressionism and especially Claude Monet's work. The latter caused the first "death" of landscape in the history of art. The most evident expression of the radical break operated by Monet is the negation of the implicit gaze, which is at the heart of pre-Impressionist painting. In his works that concern exclusively nature (especially the paintings realized in his garden at Giverny), the painter abandons frequently the horizon and any implicit somatic orientation. The usual opposition between high and low, left and right, in front and behind are now no longer valid. Monet thus adds to a first element of visual disturbance (the irritating presence of the stains of color on the canvas, stains that designate both the motif and the act of representing it) a second one: the impossibility for the viewer to orient himself *in* the painting. It cuts, so to speak, the distance necessary to the creation of the image as a traditional visual object and redefines the relation that the viewer has with the work of art. There are no more "open windows", nor landscapes to discover; the disturbing pictorial image, full of energy, requires a new approach, it appeals to the senses and the intellectual faculties of an observer confronted to the absence of a pre-existent mode of interpretation or an easily decipherable surface.

With Monet, the representation of nature becomes unstable and fluctuating. It does not crystallize in an image ready to be fixed and related—indirectly, by post-mimetic analogy—to the essential instability of nature itself. Monet tends to show what is visible to the naked eye before the intervention of intellectual abilities, pure impression, and this explains the lack of carefully balanced levels (foreground to background) in his paintings. The crisis of landscape and the development of a new form of post-landscape painting affect both the production and the reception of the work. It is well known that Monet chooses a completely artificial setting, his garden in Giverny, as the main scene of a great number of his canvases. Even this tiny corner of nature in Normandy demands endless and impossible work in order to be correctly represented. Conveying the immediacy of the impression would require an equally immediate and instant—and thus impossible— pictorial act. Seriality is both the answer (and the end of the unique work of art) and the admission of the impossibility of the project. The instability of painting, always repeated, draws it nearer to nature again, which is also in perpetual movement and transformation. Once the stasis and the usual fixity of the painting are questioned, the observer will be submitted to movement as well, especially when in front of the *kinetic* device developed by Monet at the end of his life and put on show at the Musée de l'Orangerie. The exaggerated horizontality of the paintings exhibited there force the viewer to physically create his vision by moving on (the resultant impression can never be stabilized, it exists only in and thanks to the imagination of the moving observer).[33] The nineteenth-century is considered by many historians to be the apex of the history of landscape. That same period witnesses however, beyond the deconstruction accomplished by Monet, the deep transformation of the landscape genre achieved by Paul Cézanne. The latter, like Monet, increasingly focuses his artistic journey on nature, culminating in a form of profane aesthetical reverence. Cézanne intervenes both on the painted surface and on the underlying hermeneutical structure. Some art historians have argued for the use, by the painter, of a stereoscopic device[34], which permitted to transpose a *binocular* perspective in painting. The viewer confront-

---

33. See K. Clark, *Landscape into Art*, John Murray, London 1949.
34. See A. Breidbach, *Anschauungsraum bei Cézanne und Helmholtz*, Fink, Munich 2003.

21 Paul Cézanne, *Mont Sainte Victoire*, 1902-1904, private collection

ed to Cézanne's works and eager to find the right 'angle' in order to "enter" the representation, experiences a shock in front of these highly counterintuitive compositions. Rilke describes the furious reaction of the first visitors of Cézanne's exhibitions in front of works that, to them, did not seem to represent "anything at all"[35]. Such misunderstanding is the result of the impossibility of finding a perspective, far or close, starting from which the image would appear, eventually, as stable and visible (in the usual way visibility is presented in painting). Cézanne's representations of natural scenes, in which the topical elements (trees, clouds, shrubs, etc.), recognizable as such, provide no more semantic certainties (the projection into space, subjected to doubling and fragmentation, continuously fails), mark at the same

---

35. See R.M. Rilke, *Lettres sur Cézanne* (1907); transl.: *Letters on Cézanne*, Fromm, New York 1985.

time the negation of the traditional eternal or idealized landscape. In spite of the clear absence of any action, nature here seems alive; it is life, in the sense of what has the strength to *appear*. Cézanne himself understood this surprising form of appearance as the equivalent of a landscape that "has conscience of itself"[36], while critics hinted at the synthesis between momentarily perception and artistic memory as the main cause of the effect of surprise characteristic for his paintings. The essential element, in Cézanne, is however the impenetrability of nature, which, because it appears as such, does not permit a traditional interpretation and calls for the sharpened attention of the viewer. The painted landscape therefore appears as something that, just like the empirically experienced landscape, both attracts and resists interpretation; impenetrable and untranslatable, it is the basis of an aesthetic experience, or, to put it with Henri Maldiney: "It is, every time, the unique place where we are present with all the potentialities of our body, in a mutual embrace"[37].

The surprising fact of post-mimetic and post-landscape is its constant relation with nature. The crisis of the landscape as genre implies by no means the disappearance of nature, rather the opposite. In works of painters marked by abstraction, the presence of nature is not conveyed by the landscape pattern anymore, but suggested by equivalences and associations. Nature as *kosmos*, vital force, fullness or harmony, is on the other hand directly expressed through the energy of the pictorial act. Nature lies now *within* the artist, in lives in his eye and in his hands, and therefore also in the traces he disseminates on the medium, on the condition that he allows the nature that lies in himself "to speak". The observer, no longer exposed to an identifiable theme or history, under the impact of these images of a new genre, will have to resort to his intuitive abilities rather than reason, history or knowledge. The reception of a Mondrian painting, for example, represents from this point of view both a negation of cogitation and an amplified, more complex reflection. The first effect is negative, given the impossibility to find any orientation *in* the structure on the canvas. The lack of a common spatiality creates a short-circuit; the work does not refer

---

36. "The landscape reflects itself, humanizes itself, thinks itself in me." *Peinture et vérité*, in Id., *L'art, l'éclair de l'être*, Compact, Seyssel 1993, 36.
37. H. Maldiney, *Cézanne et Sainte-Victoire*.

to something identifiable (an original idea, a recognizable pattern), nor to a hidden deep structure; it does not refer at all, limiting itself to the display of shapes and colors on canvas. It is, however, here that the associative ability of the viewer intervenes, recognizing, based on the painting itself, shapes and laws of nature presented in a non-mimetic fashion.

This briefly outlined development can easily be combined with the already mentioned formula for landscape, $L = S + N$, based on the relationship between a subject and nature. Paintings belonging to the label "landscape" exist as part of a historic field within which the relation between a privileged subject—the artist, but the viewer as well—and nature occurs. The history of landscape painting proves that it took many centuries for nature to be represented as such, as an object of pleasure worthy of attention. It is, paradoxically, only in the moment of its definitive submission to man's will, in the age of the Industrial Revolution, that nature appears in art in its bare (absence of human figures) or wild form (absence of human interventions). The "neutral" or "realistic" depiction of a Friedrich or a Constable, in search of "true" nature, nevertheless inscribes the anthropocentric blueprint of an organizing principle—it corresponds to the power of an almighty eye—in their respective works. The post-academic painting of the nineteenth-century still subordinates the object, which it intends to show without human distortion—to the dominant manner of displaying reality. It renders the reality in other words still by convention and answers to the logic of the "theatre of the world" (Maldiney). The attitude towards nature, the "strong feeling" that one encounters when looking at it, is increasingly present and claimed by the artists of that century, but it grants by no means a more direct access to it. From this point of view the subject-nature relationship at the heart of the landscape genre appears asymmetric: it is still the subjective, human point of view that has to supply the frame, the perspective and the final image of nature. The corresponding natural settings are almost invariably marked by human figures or activities and perceived from an exclusively human perspective. Pictorial landscape—the only one that has existed for many centuries before landscape became the object of an experience *in situ*—is characterized by this asymmetry, that is the dominion of the gaze of a powerful subject over nature. The theatralization or dramatization, the distancing, the framing of nature, etc. are not the inauthentic expression of a superficial approach to nature: rather, they belong to the essence of landscape itself.

Landscape as a representation and experienced landscape

Things get considerably more complicated during the eighteenth-century, when the two forms of landscape, the pictorial representation and the lived experience, begin to co-exist. Poetry—increasingly imbued with nature—, painting, the art of gardens and lived experience all influence each other. The empirical perception, possible at last, of nature *as* landscape continues to raise different interpretations. In a memorable 1964 conference, the German philosopher Joachim Ritter put forward the hypothesis that the crisis of metaphysics, caused by the development of modern natural sciences, led to the aesthetic recovery of nature understood as landscape. The new scientific objectivity and the aesthetic representation of nature are, according to him, typically modern phenomena. Landscape expresses—in art, literature, but also as a lived experience—something that escapes both science and philosophy: "What science will never be able to express is the presence of the *nature as a whole*, sky and earth, belonging to the earthly life of man as a spectacle accessible through the sense of sight"[38]. Without discussing here the validity of the new aesthetic supremacy as a substitute for the metaphysics, dethroned during the seventeenth- and the eighteenth- centuries[39], it is important to highlight, with Ritter, the concept of nature as a totality. Indeed, the new philosophy derived from the sciences, from the Renaissance onwards, laid the groundwork for a radically different approach to nature. The latter was interpreted, following an openly anti-teleological and anti-Aristotelian reading, as a reality divine in itself and self-generating. Galileo's Platonism (or Pythagorism) led him to state that the "Great Book" of nature could be read based solely on mathematic language. This perspective, clearly linked to the concept of immanence, gave nature a new dignity; hence, *all* in nature seemed worthy of attention and observation. The idea of the world's inherent order led to the idea of nature as a perfect, orderly and self-regulating machine,

---

38. J. Ritter, *Landschaft*, 157.
39. See R. Groh, D. Groh, *Weltbild und Naturaneigung,* Suhrkamp, Frankfurt am Main 1991.

which requires the study of everything, from the most minor details to the understanding of its interrelations in a system. The concept of harmony, present in Leibniz, Locke, Spinoza, and the idea of self-regulation, nature seen as a perfect clock, led to a worldview defined by philosophical optimism. The poet Alexander Pope expresses it clearly in his *Essay on Man*: "All nature is but art, unknown to thee;/ All chance, direction, which thou canst not see;/ All discord, harmony not understood;/ All partial evil, universal good"[40]. The postulate of a harmonious nature, equally present in the numerous writings of British or German *physico-theologians*, the idea according to which nature was the most faithful mirror of God, stimulated a vast literary, artistic and philosophical movement in Europe. The observation of nature, the transcription and explanation of its miracles practically became a moral obligation. Since the second half of the sixteenth-century, nature has been at the centre of the attention of sciences and philosophy. Over time, the successive theories of Copernicus, Bruno, Gilbert, Kepler, Galileo, and Newton changed the definitions of nature. Physico-theology[41] tried to prove the truth of the new approach to nature, collecting and explaining its "wonders". These factors "positivized" nature in its totality, implying, at the same time, on the aesthetic level, the acknowledgement of all its imaginable forms: not only those of beauty, but, equally, those of the picturesque and the sublime. At the time of this unprecedented symbiosis, poets (especially through descriptive poetry), painters, naturalists and philosophers all made nature "speak".

The repercussions of this enthusiastic appreciation of nature on a large scale came to us only very indirectly and mainly through written documents. The eighteenth-century has been characterized by a wide-range ideologic operation "in the search for nature". It was at that time that the act of "going out" in nature, and that of *going-towards-it*, acquired all its meaning: the deliberate action of the new "singers" of nature, poets and artists, travelers and scientists, appeared as a signal persistently oriented to nature, whose greatness and perfection were to be closely studied. The transition from ignorance to knowledge, from fear to acceptance, from observation to veneration of nature,

---

40. A. Pope, *An Essay on Man*, 1734, Epistle I, vv. 289-292.
41. See M.H. Nicolson, *Mountain Gloom and Mountain Glory. The Development of the Aesthetics of the Infinite*, Norton, New York 1959.

began in the seventeenth-century and was accomplished in the following one. The guiding concept of nature as a perfect machine, as a superstructure imposed by the philosophical, teleological, and scientific discourse, inspired and directed the urge for nature.

Thomson, Mallet, Savane, Delille, Saint-Lambert, and Haller's descriptive poetry in fact, does not just praise nature; these authors created a new language for its designation and offered at the same time several typological categories, thus laying the groundwork for the future discovery of natural beauty. Even though the attention of the period was, so to speak, drawn from nature, the visual encounter with it still roused problems. Creating an image of nature on the spot, encountering it *as* a landscape, was not something to take for granted but had to be learnt. In this regard, one of the well known theorists of Garden Art of that time, Christian L. Hirschfeld, supplies a precious testimony. He bases his reflections upon garden construction on a psychological theory that concerns the effects of landscape on the spectator. Here is his definition of landscape: "When, from the earth's vast surface, we isolate larger sections that can by themselves make up a whole, then we have landscapes"[42]. The totality, required in order to build a landscape, is not simply given at the moment of the encounter with nature. Hirschfeld underscores this aspect in another writing of 1771, *Das Landleben* (*Life in the countryside*): "The entire region surrounding us [...] was full of wonders of nature that, at first, awoke our profound admiration, but whose excessive variety overtook us to the point that we couldn't stop to admire one spectacle or the other"[43]. The reunion between subject and nature, short-circuited by the overabundance of visual data, leads to a momentary failure. The spectator finds himself in the impossibility of organizing his gaze and building an image of what goes beyond his cognitive and imaginative abilities. The creation of the visual bond with nature occurs therefore progressively, through the practice repeated on site: "Gradually, the secret pleasures of nature became more and more familiar; it seemed that they had sharpened our senses and the energies of the soul were rejuvenated"[44].

42. C.L. Hirschfeld, *Theorie der Gartenkunst*, Leipzig, 1775, vol. I, p. 188 (transl.: *Theory of Garden Art*, University of Pennsylvania Press, Philadelphia 2001, 173).
43. C.L. Hirschfeld, *Das Landleben*, Leipzig 1771, 15.
44. *Ibid.*, 16.

22 Balthasar Anton Duncker, *A Painter draws a waterfall*, 1779

The aesthetic approach, which will become popular and almost automatic during the nineteenth-century, is therefore never directly *given* (even in the case of a great enthusiast and profound expert of nature such as Hirschfeld himself), it is always the result of a process. The initial irritation in front of the impossibility of a visual appropriation turns into aesthetic pleasure once one learns how to identify specific types of natural sceneries. In fact, Hirschfeld connects specific psychological reactions to the topography of selected pieces of nature: small scattered hills provide an effect of liveliness and serenity, while forests evoke solemn greatness and composure, and so on[45]. Hence, the subject learns to be surprised by nature only after exploring it and after understanding the mechanism of the effects raised by it. This effort of *re-cognition* of nature expresses itself best via the stock of shapes (cheerful landscape, melancholic landscape, romantic landscape) mastered by the connoisseurs and increasingly popular among the large public as well.

The work of the artist Reverend William Gilpin offers another example of the enthusiastic appreciation of nature. Between 1782 and 1802, Gilpin published a series of books that explained to the British the beauty of their own country. The author taught them how to look at nature, namely the way in which the various elements found on site could be arranged into well structured and meaningful images. Gilpin's theory is based on the model of the ideal landscape and its distribution into several well-defined spaces. Real landscape, therefore, exists only when the visual data take the form of a pictorial "as if". Gilpin is the great prophet of the *picturesque* in the sense of "a term expressive of that peculiar kind of beauty, which is agreeable in a picture")[46]. Even a scholar, great traveler, and theorist of gardens like Horace Walpole had to apply the Gilpinian pictorial patterns and the lessons of the "picturesque" in order to understand the aesthetic phenomena he was looking for: "I have been an errant stroller; amusing myself by sailing down the beautiful Wye, looking at abbeys and castles, with Mr. Gilpin in my hand to teach me to criticize, and talk of foregrounds,

---

45. See W. Kehn, *Ästhetische Landschaftserfahrung und Landschaftsgestaltung in der Spätaufklärung: der Beitrag von C.C.L. Hirschfelds Gartentheorie*, in *Landschaft und Landschaften im achtzehnten Jahrhundert*, ed.: H. Wunderlich, Winter, Heidelberg 1995, 1-24.

46. W. Gilpin, *Essay on Prints*, 1768, XII.

23 William Gilpin, *Observations on the river Wye*, 1770.

and distances, and perspectives, and prominences, with all the cant of connoisseurship"[47]. At the moment of the confrontation with nature, particularly when it is wild or vast, the first reaction is astonishment and dizziness. On the one hand, the difficulty lies in situations where movement does not allow a lasting framing. At the beginning, to the traveler in search for nature, everything runs too fast before the eyes. It is necessary to learn to control the speed of the impressions, in order to freeze the visual data in a frame. The framing occurs in a situation that is different from the representations offered by panoramic devices like terraces, loggias, towers, windows, pavilions, and other buildings, which already organized the discovery of a particular view. The problem with the search for a "true" image of nature lies now in the absence or the abandonment of a predefined point of view (at least at the level of what is clear to the viewer). In the eighteenth-century, nature has above all to surprise, it has to impose itself freely. However,

47. Ann Bermingham, *System, Order and Abstraction. The Politics of English Landscape Drawing around 1795*, in *Landscape and Power*, ed.: W.J.T. Mitchell, Chicago: The University of Chicago Press, 2002, 77-101, p. 87.

even where the spectator stops in order to admire a particular prospect, things are not automatically fixed. The sight, especially from an elevated and dominant point of view, does not succeed in controlling the richness and complexity of the sensitive data. The eye is most of the time blocked or blinded, loses any control over reality. Haller formulates this very precisely in his long poem *Die Alpen*: "A sweet dizziness closes the eyes, too weak / to embrace with the sight the immense arch"[48]. The entire 18th century will serve the recovery of the control that the visual perception had lost. Regaining this power, namely the creation of aesthetically satisfying images, implies an effort of simplification and organization. This action is based primarily on the pictorial framing transposed from the dominion of painting onto nature (Gilpin's teaching), or, including specific semantic aspects, on the identification of the given data thanks to the patterns registered in the true connoisseur's imagination (Hirschfeld's approach). Such a process, which was made popular by the landscape theorists of the period and which gave rise to the generalized possibility of creating landscapes, is neither natural nor innocent. John Barrell underscored the existence of two well-defined visual traditions in eighteenth-century England: on the one hand, a traditional gaze, an "ordinary" attention, concerned only with inspecting closest realities; on the other hand, a sovereign gaze able to "gather the details in a whole"[49].

The latter disregards everything that is accidental in order to identify—from a global point of view (which mainly corresponds to the idealization found in paintings of the *ideal landscape* kind)—in what it encounters permanent, typical, and abstract aspects. Especially in the British context, the connoisseur, whose taste and supreme cognitive power was granted by financial independence and, in particular, by the possession of land, benefits from his "ability to extract from the labyrinth of nature, from the infinite variety of accidental and circumstantial phenomena, the general categories of natural beauty, whose totality is appreciated only when, on the basis of an analysis, it is possible to distinguish the different elements"[50].

48. A. von Haller, *Die Alpen*, Berne 1734.
49. J. Barrell, *The Dark Side of the Landscape: The Rural Poor in English Painting 1730-1840*, Cambridge University Press, Cambridge 1983, p. 86.
50. *Ibid.*, 87.

The successfull attempt of controlling perceivable nature refers therefore to a social position, that is an elevated point of view with political implications. The dominant bourgeoisie, founded on land ownership, asserts itself in other words through the control exercised on nature. The regard for nature as a whole and the concern to study it through all possible means, is not, therefore, a bizarre pastime; is is, rather the aesthetic complement of the conquest and definitive submission of nature. With one subtle difference, because the field of operation is no more the control of artistic representations, but that of nature itself.

The possibility of appropriating nature everywhere and in all its forms, especially those still unknown, refers moreover to the phenomenon of the sublime. The eighteenth-century was, as we all know, the great age of the discovery of the natural sublime, of the transposition of the interpretative schemes of the religious and dramatic sublime onto nature. It initially coincides with the effort performed by British intellectual-travellers during their *Grand Tour* to domesticate nature. These "tourists" actually learned to dominate the anxiety caused by alpine scenery in applying the qualities of the rhetorical sublime rediscovered and popularized by the French critic Boileau on the peaks, torrents, precipices in the Alps. The famous letter that John Dennis, 'Sir Tremendous Longinus', as his contemporaries called him, wrote in Turin in 1688 after the crossing of the Alps, bears witness to a first domestication of the rough mountain reality pursued by a subject able to interpret what, at first, resisted him.

The wild nature—that, shortly thereafter, will be identified as a sublime scenery—is, at first, a new and surprising spectacle. The first reaction, as we already said, is fear, a shock due to the confrontation with something that is unknown and impossible to understand. It is no longer something one can "read" according to established aesthetic standards. Montaigne's travels, a century earlier, provide an eloquent source in order to grasp the former way to interpret (one should rather say, not to interpret) nature. For the author of the famous *Essais*, who crossed several times the Alps, "the most pleasant landscape he had ever seen" meant simply to identify a type of cultural landscapes where the (chaotic) topography became something orderly (that is landscape) thanks to the human traces disseminated on site.

> Beyond this we came upon a valley of great extent through which the Inn flows to join the Danube at Vienna. In Latin it is called

Oenus. It is five or six days' journey by water from Insprug to Vienna. To M. de Montaigne this valley seemed the fairest country he had ever seen, now narrowing itself with the mountains pressing close on it, now spreading out wide on our side of the river the left and forming a space meet for cultivation on the very slopes of the mountains, which were not too steep for this, and now expanding on the other bank. Next it would reveal to the eye platforms on two or three different levels, one above the other, and everywhere fair houses of noblemen and churches. And all this in a country shut and walled in on every side by mountains of immeasurable height[51].

Montaigne's eye follows names, buildings, historical traces and he visually fixes the distances between things; he is focused on human activities; he enjoys the "pleasant" territory, pleasant and livable because it already functions as a place where life thrives (farming, working, construction). We can find a very similar perspective in a great humanist of the sixteenth-century, Francesco Guicciardini. During his trip to Spain he writes:

> We left on the fourth from Figueres and arrived at Girona, five leagues away, in the evening [...] the place is ill-inhabited, mountainous and not very domestic; the city is built on a hill [...] On the fifth we left Girona and, under the snow, came to Sterlich, another five leagues away; the castle is of poor quality; and the land is wild and unpleasant. From what I've seen of Ragona, it is a sterile, uncultivated, almost deserted town and it also is a poor land, in shortage of water.[52]

Piero Camporesi underlines justly: "Nothing was farther from the taste of the sixteenth century than a purely natural landscape—one that wasn't created and built by human clever industriousness—a free open space, uncultivated, a *land* that wasn't deeply marked by the presence of man and his various arts, his industry, his artifice"[53]. While Montaigne and Guicciardini traverse primarily domesticated territories, Dennis ventures into "mountains of

---

51. *Journal de voyage de Michel de Montaigne*, ed.: F. Rigolot, PUF, Paris 1992, 50 (transl.: *The journal of Montaigne's travels in Italy: by way of Switzerland and Germany in 1580 and 1581*, J. Murray, London 1903, 158.
52 *Ibid*.

immeasurable height", where such work has not taken place yet: "the unusual height in which we found our selves, the impending Rock that hung over us, the dreadful Depth of the Precipice, and the Torrent that roar'd at the bottom, gave us such a view as was altogether new and amazing"[54]. As most of the other travelers of his time confronted to wild nature, Dennis faces something that resists him, a reality that, at first, is *unbearable*, impossible to frame and to capture as an image.

The approach to nature which is characteristic of the second half of the seventeenth-century appears therefore as a contradictory challenge: the modern subject (the erudite traveler who already knows that the *whole* nature is worthy of interest and has to be explored) studies nature, he desires to visually occupy the totality of the earth but, once exposed to the power of nature, he does not cease to notice his own weakness. At least free (the *new sciences*, philosophy, and *physico-theology* have paved the way and legitimized his venture into nature), the subject is still frustrated, since his gaze cannot bear what he himself craved to discover. It is this very peculiar "mixed feeling", theorized by the intellectuals of that period, that will allow Dennis to apply the rhetorical sublime on nature on the basis of the mixed or oxymoronic reaction before a wild nature: "The sense of all of this produc'd different motions in me, *viz.*, a delightful Horror, a terrible Joy, and at the same time, I was infinitely pleas'd, I trembled"[55]. Let us not forget that between 1680 and 1690, when Dennis discovered the surprising effects of savage nature, the ideal was clearly still that of the garden-nature, as stated in Saint-Évremond's *Dissertation sur le mot de Vaste*:

---

53. P. Camporesi, *Le belle contrade. Nascita del paesaggio italiano,* Garzanti, Milan 1992, 9-10.
54. J. Dennis, *The Critical Works*, ed.: E. Niles Hooker, The Johns Hopkins University Press, Baltimore 1939-43, vol. II, 380.
55. *Ibid.*

> The vast forests scare us, the sight dissolves and gets lost looking at the vast countryside. [...] The wild countries that haven't been cultivated yet, those ruined by the desolation of the war, the deserted and abandoned lands, there is something vast about them that arouses a secret feeling of horror in us [...] vast is more or less equal to broken, ruined.[56]

During the eighteenth-century, landscape will gain a considerable place in the system of aesthetics: it will function at the same time as the means and as the result of a new approach to nature, which became essential once its totality demanded to be acknowledged. This development debuts, as we have seen, with a race towards the unknown, with the powerful call of a nature still considered as virgin; the next step will consist in the countless explorations and travels of that time, the poetic discoveries of nature via walks or journeys (Coleridge and Wordsworth come to mind). While the philosophic discourse required the most accurate description and an exhaustive poeticization of nature, contemporary economics and politics dealt with the annexation of nature by other means. At the beginning, however, the access to nature invariably lead to an insuperable shock, linked to two causes: the radical novelty of the encountered reality and the influence of the traditional patterns permitting the interpretation of nature. The German poet and physico-theologian Brockes suggests therefore in his poem *Bewährtes Mittel für die Augen*:

> In a flat and open field in which you go walking,/ And given the lack of stimuli, you see nothing but fields and the sky,/ I want to show you a thousand landscapes of different beauty instead of one./ You simply have to fold up one of your hands/ And hold it before your eyes as it was a telescope;/ So that, through the small opening, part of the things you see/ A part of the landscape, is transformed into a personal landscape./ So much that—if one is a painter—one could draw or paint/ a really nice depiction.[57]

---

56. Saint-Evremond, *Œuvres en prose*, ed.: R. Ternois, Marcel Didier, Paris 1966, vol. III, 375-417.

57. H. Brockes, *Irdisches Vergnügen in Gott,* Kissner, Hamburg 1727, vol. V, 623.

24 T. Gainsborough, *The Man Holding a Claude Glass,* Yale Center for British Art

The initial frustration (at first there is nothing to see but simple scattered elements, "fields and sky") asks for an effort carried out here by the hand transformed into a telescope. The optical instrument delimits, unifies and specifies the data and thus generates aesthetic images, works of art *in nuce*. What Brockes illustrates through a simple gesture that allows the production of images of nature, that is landscapes, will actually require several decades. The victory of the subject over nature, which has for a long time resisted becoming an image, will have as a consequence the assertion of the self that operates this translation; the subject enjoys his own power, the intellectual work carried out on nature, and the methods and inventions discovered on the road. He gives meaning to nature, which he dominates thanks to the landscape experience. "Such a place that, without resorting to our researches, would just be a dreadful and sterile place, will, from now on, become alive and it will make nature and history speak"[58]. Thus Jean-Pierre Papon expressed himself in 1780. The sublime seems in this context the paradigmatic territory of the subject, given that what causes anxiety and frustration, the strongest feelings, is followed by the highest self-enjoyment. Experiencing a form of (pure, wild) nature, which he will declare sublime, the subject accomplishes a sort of second Creation: he searches for the unusual and the surprising, and, once he overcomes his anxiety, he finally transforms everything he discovered on site into strong images. The universal victory over nature potentially implies the end of terror; in order to find natural realities that cause sublime reactions, the subject will have to move on and always look for new objects. Yet, at the end of the eighteenth-century, almost everything is discovered and under the control of the intellect, and the anxiety and the chance of being touched by the sublime disappear. The "final victory" over nature has unexpected consequences: once under visual control, transformable anywhere and anytime in a series of forceful landscapes, nature does no longer arouse interest. This explains why the moment of the most unbridled research of sublime or picturesque spectacles, in the years around 1800, coincides with a frustrating feeling of *déjà-vu*, that is the circulation of landscapes far too similar to each other, repeated over and over again.

58. J.-P. Papon, *Voyage littéraire en Provence*, Barrois l'ainé, Paris 1780, XIII.

The Romantic poet Clemens Brentano expresses with much irony this state of affairs in his novel *Godwi* (1798-1800): "This whole valley is now the image of an endeavor that has suddenly stopped, everything demands an ending, and one could say that it is an interesting story that has been interrupted right in the middle by a question mark"[59]. The automatism of the landscape process and the success of the aesthetic *Bildung* have reached a point in which the images begin to devaluate the encounter with nature.

The failure of the landscape consciousness in the moment of its greatest historical triumph will have significant repercussions. It paves the way for the absolute subjectivity of the Romantic and Idealist movements, in other words for the invention of an infinitely powerful inner nature and of artificial paradises, leading therefore to an estrangement from nature[60]. Imagination, which already came to power during the conquest of sublime nature, becomes autonomous and generates entire "worlds" by itself. Jean Paul Richter's literary landscapes illustrate this perfectly:

> The enchanted ring of the horizon at sunset was laying upon her like a shining wheel of fire—her eyes looked down towards the peaks that were bright green. The vast oratory of the earth was surrounded by green blends—and upon them the movements of a storm with sparkles everywhere was raising from the purplish arena and the wheel of fire of the horizon and, through all of this, the hustle of a forest without the echo of the thunder—and the quiet eye of the sun was veiled by the sheet of rain of the storm. The cloud didn't open any waterfall but only a tepid Staubbach on the autumn blanket of the earth, and instead of the wavy line and spark of the lightning, the whole fog bank was illuminated only by the shimmer of the oil lamp[61].

The defeat in question keeps pace with the weakening of the Kantian aesthetics of nature: it opens a void that exists up to the present day, and indeed after Kant there is no longer an aesthetic of nature

---

59. C. Brentano, *Godwi*, Reclam, Stuttgart 1995, 343.
60. See O. Bätschmann, *Entfernung der Natur, Landschaftsmalerei 1750-1920*, Dumont, Cologne 1989.
61. J. P. Richter, *Der Jubelsenior, Werke*, Hanser, Munich 1968, vol. IV, 426.

worthy of its name. The brief cultural season of the eighteenth century, during which nature was visually interesting to such an extent that it led to a collective obsession, thus comes to an end. From this moment onwards the return to nature via landscape is frequently linked to the idea of the loss or destruction of nature, whether it is in Ruskin or Rudorff in the nineteenth-century, or in McHarg in the twentieth.

Landscape—the successful transformation of the perception of a piece of nature into an image—is the result of immediacy and cultural mediation at the same time, of surprise and conquest, simultaneity and composition. Its ambiguity will also have significant repercussions in the field of art. The attempts of Friedrich, Constable, Monet or Cézanne—all characterized by a "strong feeling in front of nature"—to finally render nature as such, suggest the paradoxical recovery of landscape through art. Painting has been for many centuries the exclusive place of the encounter with nature—Chateaubriand said: "The landscape is on Claude Lorrain's palette, not on the Campo Vaccino"[62] —until when, in the eighteenth-century, the encounter finally happened *in* the subject himself and no longer in or through artistic artefacts. The same period was also, as we know, that of the generalized venture into nature, of its celebration, which culminated, among other things, in the invention of the irregular or picturesque garden[63]. When Kant claimed the primacy of nature over art, the lived experience of nature felt by a subject on site, such a statement could appear, for a moment, as a provocation: the real life was now "outside", in the direct contact with nature, which could be transformed into beautiful, sublime or picturesque landscapes. Once the ambiguities of the landscape and the *projective* activity of the subject became clear, and exposed to *cliché*-landscapes, the conscience of nature returned again in the domain of art.

---

62. F.-R. de Chateaubriand, *Mémoires d'outre-tombe,* Folio, Paris 1973, vol. III, 72 (transl.: *The memoirs of Chateaubriand*, Alfred A. Knopf, New York 1961).

63. See J. Dixon Hunt, *The Picturesque Garden in Europe*, Thames & Hudson, London 2003.

CHAPTER V

FROM
THE PICTURESQUE
TO THE POSTMODERN

In the eighteenth-century, philosophy also started to explore the complexity of the reception of nature as landscape. The difficulty to provide an account of it, even a brief one, is due to the double perspective of the aesthetic approach: the theorists of the time tried to give a general explanation of the aesthetic pleasures offered by beautiful, sublime or picturesque landscapes. These philosophical positions are however linked to a moment in history in which the approach to nature was not only a scientific problem, but one that concerned the scholarly public in general and a certain praxis. Theories, fashions, descriptive categories and the main concepts applied to the different forms of nature are therefore not external to the aesthetic practice; they partly take place within it.

We already mentioned the starting point and the fundamental contradiction of the visual encounter with nature: it occurs when imagination comes into play in order to give meaning to the inanimate material transmitted by the senses and to transform it into landscape, source of aesthetic pleasure. The initial difficulty, the shock in front of the (immeasurable) nature, leaves space to a process that allows, gradually, to acknowledge or appreciate the given object. While a beautiful nature arouses standard associations, the sublime nature still has to be domesticated and identified in order to be considered as an object of aesthetic pleasure. Imagination thus acts as a powerful amplifier, which allows one to go beyond the primary or immediate effects of perception, generating secondary effects according to the principle of analogy or proximity. Analogy gives, for example, the possibility of "seeing" an image of youth or life in a spring-like landscape, while the principle of proximity gives rise to almost infinite individual associations. In the encounter with beautiful or sublime nature, the natural reality contemplated on the spot is therefore often an excuse for the assertion of the *Self* and its imaginative and intellectual abilities.

Now, in a period that fully experienced the disintegration of classical aesthetics, the beautiful risked, , invariably, to annoy, while the sublime, recently conquered and part of the aesthetic education, tired. The picturesque, made popular and taught on site by William Gilpin, Uvedale Price or Richard Payne Knight, already represented, from this point of view, an *Ersatz*, an answer to the crisis of the landscape gaze exposed to mechanized spontaneity. The picturesque

25 *Le Touriste*, Revue (1866)

is the negation of the the beautiful and the sublime (the only ones that Kant recognized) or, better, according to its promoters, a more elevated form[1]. The picturesque attracts the gaze of the viewer for itself, it is the *immediate* effect that the glimpse of nature has on him: "Nor is there in travelling a greater pleasure, than when a scene of grandeur bursts unexpectedly upon the eye, accompanied with some accidental circumstance of the atmosphere, which harmonizes with it, and gives it double value»[2]. The picturesque can be an old ruined tower in the middle of a bucolic site, an abandoned cottage, solitary villages and paths. The picturesque acts by contrast, asymmetry, through the surprise it arouses, but also simply thanks to what an eye trained to the picturesque brings about:

> We seek it [the picturesque] among all the ingredients of landscape—trees—rocks—broken grounds—woods—rivers—lakes—plains—vallies—mountains—and distances. These objects *in themselves* produce infinite variety. No two rocks, or trees are exactly the same. They are varied, a second time, by *combination*; and almost as much, a third time, by different *lights, and shades*, and other aerial effects.[3]

Towards the end of the eighteenth-century, when the beautiful and the sublime seem to be no longer able to arouse the expected emotions, the receptive situation reverses: while the venture into nature began between surprises and shock, now, given the situation caused by the overabundance of beautiful and sublime images, it is the surprise *as such* that is sought. The picturesque appears in other terms as the overcoming of the beautiful and the sublime. Even associations, ideas and reflections, made possible by the encounter with nature, seem secondary and repetitive if compared to the direct approach to the source of aesthetic pleasures. According to its promoters, the picturesque has an immediate effect and supplies, every time, new images of nature. It thus represents both an illusion (a further variation of the visual access to nature) and an alternative (a new reality).

1. "Picturesqueness, therefore, appears to hold a station between beauty and sublimity; and on that account, perhaps, is more frequently and more happily blended with them both than they are with each other. It is, however, perfectly distinct from either." (U. Price, *Essay on the Picturesque*, Robson, London 1794, 90).
2. W. Gilpin, *Three Essays on Picturesque Beauty*. London 1794, Essay II, *On Picturesque Travel* 90.
3. *Ibid.*, 91.

An illusion, already indicated by the term itself, *picturesque*, namely, "worthy of being painted" or "like a painting". The sense of disorder, difference and non-similarity induced by the different elements of the picturesque landscape is far from being natural or merely given. It is based, at a minimum, on the presence of identifiable signs, often anthropomorphic and, at a maximum, on a disposition that actually reduces landscape to a scene set for the fortuitous encounter between some symbolic entities. The gaze that lingers on picturesque scenes is, in itself, equally predefined. It is a search for surprising sensations that leads to the development—a well-established and documented trend—of actual "picturesque travels".[4]

The alternative to the commercial or organized touring consists in this same gaze that, once "assimilated", is capable to find nevertheless unlimited targets in reality. The selection is based, of course, on a rather limited catalogue of elements worthy of creating a picturesque assemblage: ruins of any kind, cottages, solitary trees, etc. Gilpin and Price, however, suggest the possibility of self-censoring the semantical or formal associations, always tributary of a given period, and favoring instead the play of light, proportions, chromatic qualities or any component suitable for the creation of contrasts. The picturesque becomes thus, in its most radical form, the surprising landscape *tout court*. When the subject succeeds in giving up or suppressing knowledge for a moment, the picturesque, as a new aspect of nature, seems to be able to entrust—*in extremis*—images that are not yet framed, compromised, fixed or identified[5], to him. The search for the picturesque appears therefore to be an extreme effort to retrieve innocence, to recapture the first and most powerful effect of the image of nature.

Starting from the nineteenth-century, the creation of landscapes on site is threatened by different factors. First of all, the highly ideological operation of the assessment of national territories that was in action. England, which is undergoing an unprecedented literary and pictorial campaign of a "seizing of images", is once again at the forefront. The touring and its verbal and iconic representation on a large scale refer, in other words, to openly political and economic purposes.

4. See M. Price, *The Picturesque Moment*, in *From Sensibility to Romanticism. Essays Presented to Frederick A. Pottle*, ed.: F.W. Hilles, H. Bloom, Oxford University Press, Oxford-New York 1965, 259-292.

5. Novelty—an essential concept of the aesthetics of the picturesque—exists, however, only in relation to something else.

The aesthetics of landscape, and the activities of viewing and displaying English places through which it was experienced, created for those who could participate in it a claim on England as their national aesthetics property. What began in the eighteenth century with the improvement, display and representation of private property quickly gave birth to a concept of public property. [...] by 1810 Wordsworth speaks of the Lake District as "a sort of national property" for the "persons of pure taste" who admire and visit it. Where England is "a sort of national property" for the landscape viewer, such "persons of pure taste" in effect constitute the nation.[6]

Another important factor of the time is the panorama, the triumph of popular panoramic spectacles. Their success actually underscores an important change: thanks to them, the image of nature actually returned *into* the city, birthplace of the gaze that led once to its own discovery. In a panorama, the operating point of view is hyper-anthropomorphic[7], since the presented view is nothing more than a technical assembly made up of various pieces. The taste for panoramas actually replaces real contexts, difficult to access, and offers a powerful image independent from the contingencies of the outside world. It also allows, thanks to technology, to go beyond the limitations of framing. Sublime or picturesque landscapes, when they reach their effect, function, let us not forget, as fixed and stabilized images. The dynamic effect occurs only within the imagination: the subject goes beyond the image, leaving space to the "unlimited power of fancy in multiplying and varying the objects, the results, and the gratifications of our pursuits beyond the bounds of reality, or the probable duration of existence"[8]. Circular panoramas, instead, allow to actually split the painting, creating the illusion of an infinite landscape, that absolute vision held dear by the Romantics.

The primacy of the iconic (technological) representation is equally manifest in the field of applied arts. From the nineteenth-century, landscapes on wallpapers become increasingly popular. They carry

6. E. Helsinger, *Turner and the Representation of England*, in W.J.T. Mitchell, *Landscape and Power*, 105-106.
7. See H. Makowski, B. Buderath, *Die Natur dem Menschen untertan. Ökologie im Spiegel der Landschaftsmalerei*, Kindler, Munich 1983, 129.
8. R.P. Knight, quoted in W.J. Wipple, *The Beautiful, the Sublime and the Picturesque in Eighteenth-Century British Aesthetic Theory*, Southern Illinois University Press, Carbondale 1975, 277.

26 Caspar Wolf, *Bridge and gorge of Dala River at Leukerbad*, 1774-1777, Sion Fine Arts Museum

the image of nature inside bourgeois houses even better than the complicated and exceptional panoramic devices and thus signify the annexation of the sublime and picturesque corners of the entire world. The panoramic wallpaper *Vues de Suisse* (1820), for example, was based on a model made up of 1,024 wooden planks.[9] The work brings together in a huge collage the most characteristic elements of Switzerland: the Matterhorn and the Furka Pass, the Devil's Bridge and the Staubbach Waterfall, the clefts of St. Gotthard and the Bernese farmhouses. Another factory sold, in the same years, wallpapers depicting "the savages of the Pacific". The manufacturer praised his work emphasizing that "without leaving his house and by only looking in front of himself, an active man who reads travel guides and travelers' journals will feel in the company of those same characters."[10] The new technique of the wallpaper shows the world close at hand while removing the sense of displacement and making immediacy useless.

The last example concerns the landscape genre and its uses. Towards 1774, the Bernese gallerist Abraham Wagner commissioned Caspar Wolf to paint a series of 200 alpine landscapes[11]. The artist studied carefully several Alpine sites and made sketches on the spot, during the summer, from 1774 to 1778, transposing his impressions and notes in his Bernese studio into paintings with the standard size of 82 x 54 cm. Wagner conceived these typical views of the , mostly vast landscapes of glaciers, as unsellable prototypes displayed to the public. It was possible to commission copies of different sizes or just settle for colored incisions.

Panoramas and picturesque or sublime wallpapers extend over the field of landscape. Only the boundless landscape seems to correspond to the expectations of a romantic subject who, at this point, thinks that the true infinite exists only within the imagination:

> Nature in itself as an object of perception is neither sublime nor infinite, since all of its components are separated, at least visually. The sea, with its mists and dawns, cannot be embraced in just one gaze, the sky is indefinable with its light-blue and the

---

9. See S. Thümmler, *Landschaftsmotive im Innenraum. Bemerkungen zur Panoramatapete um 1800,* in *Landschaft und Landschaften im achtzehnten Jahrhundert,* ed.: H. Wunderlich, Winter, Heidelberg 1995, 157-178.

10. *Ibid.*, 127.

abysses with their darkness. However, the sea, the sky and the abyss are sublime, not for the gift of the senses, but thanks to the fantasy, which overcomes every optical limit [...] and allows the gaze to penetrate what is truly without limits.[12]

The serial production of scenic wallpapers with landscape or alpine patterns destroys, at the same time, the concept of the original: the image of nature has become technically reproducible and a merchandise.

All these factors indicate reveal the extreme pressures exercised on landscape. The supreme danger lies of course in the idea that everything is already mapped and therefore there is nothing else to see. In *Bouvard et Pécuchet*, Gustave Flaubert's posthumous novel, this ambiguity is dealt with great sensibility and perspicacity. Landscape is not directly the theme of the book, since its two rather ridiculous protagonists do not travel at all, and their knowledge of the world, despite their universal ambitions, is only based on literature. In the attempt of creating a garden, following the most progressive precepts of that time, the aesthetic of nature will become of the utmost importance for Bouvard and Pécuchet. The two, reading some manuals, find a repertoire of well-established styles, ready to be reproduced:

> Fortunately, they discovered amongst their collection of books Boitard's work entitled *L'Architecte des Jardins*. The author divides them into a great number of styles. First there is the melancholy and romantic style, which is distinguished by immortelles, ruins, tombs, and "a votive offering to the Virgin, indicating the place where a lord has fallen under the blade of an assassin." The terrible style is composed of overhanging rocks, shattered trees, burning huts; the exotic style, by planting Peruvian torch-thistles, "in order to arouse memories in a colonist or a traveler". The grave style should, like Ermenonville, offer a temple to philosophy. The majestic style is character-

11. See Y. Boerlin-Brodbeck. *Die Entdeckung der Alpen in der Landschaftsmalerei des 18. Jahrhunderts*, in *Landschaft und Landschaften*, 253-270.
12. J.P. Richter, *Über die natürliche Magie der Einbildungskraft*, in Id., *Kleinere erzählende Schriften*, Hanser, Munich 1962, 201.

ized by obelisks and triumphal arches; the mysterious style by moss and by grottoes; while a lake is appropriate to the dreamy style. There is even a fantastic style, of which the most beautiful specimen might have been lately seen in a garden at Würtemberg—for there might have been met successively a wild boar, a hermit, several sepulchers, and a barque detaching itself from the shore of its own accord, in order to lead you into a boudoir where water-spouts lave you when you are settling yourself down upon a sofa.[13]

The two amateur gardeners will only imitate a common practice, the realization of landscape effects based on pre-existent models (an attitude that Goethe had already criticized in his reconstruction of the picturesque garden craze of the second half of the eighteenth century in *Elective Affinities*). Everything, including nature, has already been identified and catalogued. Bouvard and Pécuchet live thus in an era in which all is deposited, grouped, labeled; knowledge itself creates a huge encyclopedic storage, a big warehouse where cultural values are stacked on top of each other.

The repertoire of the possible styles to which the Flaubertian anti-heroes refer is based on two real examples of the period. Beyond Boitard's work, they allude to Gabriel Thouin who, in 1820 already, in his *Plans raisonnés de toutes les espèces de jardins,* wrote an exhaustive catalogue of everything that was available in the field of the art of gardens. (Thouin even suggested the construction of a huge domain around Versailles, containing a miniature catalogue of the most important parks of the world.) The garden of Flaubert's novel, once finished, becomes the object of a collective burlesque reception:

> Almost immediately [...] they uncorked the champagne, whose detonations caused an additional sense of enjoyment. Pécuchet made a sign; the curtains opened, and the garden showed itself. In the twilight it looked dreadful. The rockery, like a mountain, covered the entire grass plot; the tomb formed a cube in the midst of spinaches, the Venetian bridge a circumflex accent over the kidney-beans, and the summer-house beyond a big black spot, for they had burned its straw roof to make it more poetic.

13. G. Flaubert, *Bouvard et Pécuchet,* Gallimard, Paris 1979, 21 (transl.: *Bouvard and Pécuchet,* Dodo Press, Boston 2009).

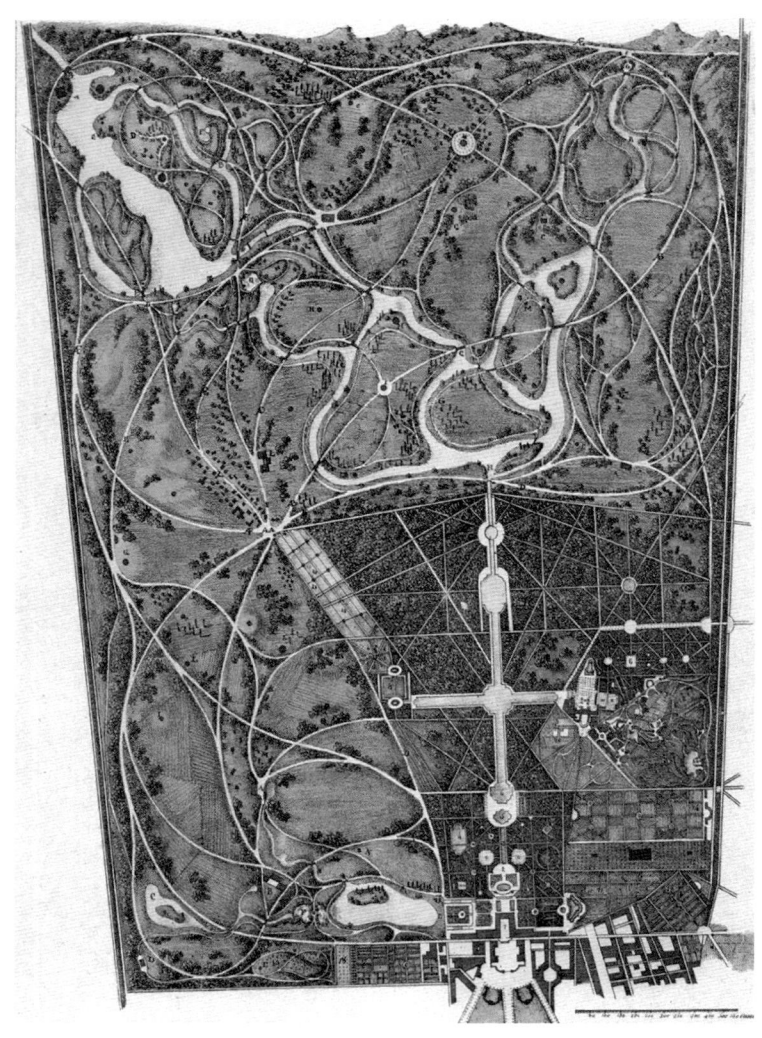

27 Gabriel Thouin, *Plans raisonnés de toutes les espèces de jardins*, Paris 1820

> The yew trees, shaped like stags or armchairs, succeeded to the tree that seemed thunder-stricken, extending transversely from the elm row to the arbour, where tomatoes hung like stalactites. Here and there a sunflower showed its yellow disk. The Chinese pagoda, painted red, seemed a lighthouse on the hillock. The peacocks' beaks, struck by the sun, reflected back the rays, and behind the railed gate, now freed from its boards, a perfectly flat landscape bounded the horizon.[14]

Flaubert's caricatured deconstruction must not make us forget the essential: the certainty of living in a time where every style of every period can be documented, imitated and mixed at will. Bouvard and Pécuchet's situation is therefore precisely a postmodern one: the end of history as a succession of meaningful innovations and the debut of the syncretic aesthetic of the mixture, the assemblage, and the *pastiche*.[15] Now, this situation of crisis—where everything is nothing but a remake, an eclectic *remix* of previous cultural forms—is exactly what the experience of landscape experienced as a less and less authentic phenomenon teaches. It should be sufficient to consider from this point of view the most venerated target of the European landscape gaze, the . High mountains, true cult objects and ground of the collective experience of the Self during the second half of the eighteenth-century, turn into a reality that will make the aesthetic reception increasingly difficult.

Chateaubriand provides evidence of this in his travel journal of 1805, *Le Mont Blanc, paysages de montagne*. His frontal attack on the most prominent object of aesthetic desire, the Mont Blanc, culminates in the following assertion:

> The idea of great sublimity is attached to mountainous views, and with justice as far as regards the grandeur of objects; but if it be proved that this grandeur, though real, is not properly perceived by the senses, what becomes of the sublimity? It is with the monuments of nature as with those of art. To enjoy their beauty, a person must be stationed at the true point of

---

14. *Ibid.*, 28.
15. See F. Jameson, *Postmodernism, or the Culture and Logic of Late Capitalism*, in «New Left Review», July-August 1984, 146, 59-92.

28 John Ruskin, *The Valley of Lauterbrunnen*, around 1866

perspective. Without this the forms, the colouring, and the proportions entirely disappear.[16]

In his "critique of the mountains", Chateaubriand faces the dominant artificial and standardized aestheticization of his time. Alpine landscape has been 'covered' around 1800 with a thick blanket of meanings, with the mountains as a vast text, a palimpsest of successive descriptions, to the point that the critical observer doesn't find anything interesting to discover. Chateaubriand, during his anti-tour, deconstructs both the sublime and the picturesque. The "cozy landscape" and its topical elements, such as alpine *chalets*, never move him: "I have not been able to discover in these *chalets*, rendered famous by the enchanting imagination of J.-J. Rousseau, anything but miserable huts filled with the ordure of cattle, and the smell of cheese and fermented milk".[17] Even the traveler's imagination, true source of aesthetic pleasure, according to the theories in vogue, remains stuck: "Those who have discovered diamonds,

16. F.-R. de Chateaubriand, *Voyage au Mont-Blanc* (transl.: *Journey to Mont Blanc*, in Id., *Travels in America and Italy*, vol. II., H. Colburn, London 1828, 330.

17. *Ibid.*, 336.

topazes, and emeralds, in the glaciers, are more fortunate than I was; my imagination was never able to perceive these treasures.»."[18]

The referential system invoked by Chateaubriand, painting, is completely anachronistic. The alpine spectacle is a "theatre", in which one must occupy the right place in order for everything to look like a successful "painting": "For every painting a canvas is necessary; in nature, the sky is the canvas to the landscape; if that be wanting in the back-ground, everything is confused and without effect".[19] By facing such landscapes, the travelers of the picturesque and the sublime, criticized by Chateaubriand, appear to be the victims of a form of illusion or voluntary blindness, motivated not by what they see but the naïve appropriation of omnipresent *tableaux*. The domesticated territory of the alpine valleys, where one feels compelled to admire the landscapes ("All I require is, that I may not be compelled to admire the long list of rocks, quagmires, chasms, holes, and contortions of the Alpine valleys[20]"), allows only two ambiguous escape routes: to search for the farthest perspective point, in order to enclose the totality in a finally satisfying image or "seek, upon the Tabor and the Taygetus, fresh colours and fresh harmonies, after having painted the inglorious hills and unknown valleys of the New World".[21]

Obermann, a novel published by Senancour, in 1804, equally proves the increasing difficulties of the disenchanted observer's correct approach to nature. The eponymous hero, a stateless post-revolutionary who lives in boredom and extreme solitude, tries to find a handhold to nature during a life with "no projects". Along an itinerary meant as an "anti-travel", he will only know defection after defection: nature does not talk to his imagination ("Why is it that Nature so seldom offers what imagination suggests to our desires?"[22]) and will gradually disappear in a meteorological "mist":

> Vapours rose insensibly from the glaciers and formed clouds under my feet. The snowy brilliance no longer tired my eyes, and the sky became still more sombre, still more profound. A

18. *Ibid.*, 332.
19. *Ibid.*, 334.
20. *Ibid.*, 344.
21. *Ibid.*; see also D. Bunn, «*Our Wattled Cot*»: Mercantile and Domestic Space in Thomas Pringle's African Landscapes, in Mitchell, *Landscape and Power*, 148-153.
22. E. P. Senancour, *Oberamann*, ed.: A. E. Waite, P. Wellby, London 1903, 29.

29 John Ruskin, *The Aiguille Blaitière,* 1856

mist covered the Alps; some isolated peaks alone issued from that sea of vapours; brilliant streaks of snow retained in their rugged clefts made the granite masses more black and austere by contrast. The hoary dome of Mont Blanc lifted its irremovable mass above that ashen and shifting ocean, above those crowded hazes rent by winds and cast up in immense billows. A black point showed suddenly in their abysses, rapid in motion, coming straight toward me; it was the mighty eagle of the Alps, with dripping wings and ravenous eye, seeking for prey, but at the sight of man he took flight with an ominous scream, and casting himself into the clouds, he vanished.[23]

While the landscape chromatically turns from blinding white to dark shades (grey, black) and the majestic heights (clouds, clefts) give way to the abyss, the visual channel altogether is replaced by the sounds of the violent wind and the "ominous scream" of a solitary bird. In Senancour's post-baroque vision, nature becomes hostile again and exposes the isolated wanderer to his finitude and existential angst. The high mountain, the privileged scenery of

23. *Ibid.,* 41.

"sublime feelings" during the eighteenth century, is no longer a place where to encounter nature, at least on the immediate level of visual perception; it is, here, rather the scene where the subject is excluded. For Obermann, nature creates "discordance" and appears as a spectacle that is definitively obsolete: "Favourable climates, scenes of beauty, nocturnal skies, pregnant sounds, old memories, seasons, opportunity, Nature eloquent in her loveliness, sublime affections, all these have passed before me, all invoke me, and all abandon me [24]". At the end of his journey, the mountainous region itself becomes "hideous" to Obermann, who, completely disenchanted but lucid, acknowledges the radical distance which divides him from nature.

With his melancholy character's ineffective journey, Senancour anticipates the "setting of the romantic sun" (Baudelaire). Chateaubriand's anti-journey, the example of Senancour's Obermann, Clemens Brentano's and Ludwig Tieck's ironic deconstructions, Jean Paul Richter's and E.T.A. Hoffmann's landscapes of pure phantasy, etc.—all of this indicates, at the beginning of a century that will witness the increase in interest for nature on a quantitative level an evident qualitative impoverishment. Landscape becomes a commercial value, a resource like any other. In general terms, the nineteenth-century will be the age of the territorial and social expansion of landscape. The first occurs through the application of landscape patterns to exotic realities. The patterns initially elaborated "at home" are transposed to the colonies and, later on, to the entire world. In this regard it is worthwhile to note that the idea of Switzerland, the privileged destination of picturesque and sublime tourism, will be exported, with the result of the creation of up to 116 other "Switzerlands" around the world.[25] The *here* and the *elsewhere* thus meet in the *topos* of Helvetia. Regarding landscape, the typically postmodern attitude does not distinguish between the original and the copy; on the contrary, it allows the invention of countless interesting territories, none of which is truly new (the Pyrenees, for example, were 'discovered' because of their resemblance with typical Alpine categories[26]).

24. *Ibid.*, 81.
25. See I. Siedentop, *Die Schweizen – eine fremdenverkehrsgeographische Dokumentation*, in *Zeitschrift für Wirtschaftsgeographie*, 1984, 28, 126-130.
26. S. Briffaud, *Naissance d'un paysage. La montagne pyrénéenne à la croisée des regards, XVIe -XIXe siècles*, AGM/AHP, Tarbes-Toulouse 1994.

The economic momentum allows the number of actual viewers, travelers and hikers of any kind to grow endlessly. With them, or rather, in order to let them circulate, a growing number of images circulate around the world, too. The image thus replaces the reality (the panoramic shows and the high quality illustrations actually substitute their referent, the real places), transforms it (architecture and the design of resorts are at the service of the picturesque, they create a new topography) or recreates it in the minds of the people. The amazing increase in the demand for landscape should not eclipse however the essential: the traveler knows by now that wherever he goes he will find only what he brought there himself, and that the solitary places he has not discovered yet, Chateaubriand's "New Worlds", tend to disappear, because, if anything, they will be read according to the same patterns applied to the already-domesticated territories.

A different attitude towards landscape?

Is it possible to imagine a different way of accessing nature, that is a less ambiguous form of landscape?

The difference we have in mind, the fact of resisting imposed models and a society of landscape consumerism implies awareness, be it voluntary or involuntary. At a certain historical moment, artists chose definitely the voluntary way: they intended to redefine the way of looking at nature altogether (Constable even wanted to "forget he ever saw a painting"[27] and presented a type of representation that resisted tradition and the dictatorship of academic painting. Friedrich's innovations, together with those of Turner, Constable or Cézanne (who would state: "the landscape has never been painted") expanded the cognitive and aesthetic horizon and caused, by means of their transgressions, true visual shocks. Our perception changes if we look at nature *after* seeing these works. Samuel Taylor Coleridge—the English poet who, between 1794 and 1834, crossed different European regions and wrote down his impressions in his famous *Notebooks*—was following a transgressive path quite similar to those of the above-mentioned painters. In fact, he wanted to

27. ***The Notebooks of Samuel Taylor Coleridge***, ed. K. Coburn, Routledge & Kegan Paul, London 1957, note 1489.

look at nature for what it was, without the intervention of topical cultural patterns. He exposed himself to the reality in an extreme, even painful way "My eyes are tired[28]. His prose is, at the same time, the stuttering shorthand that traces the initial impression, and the perpetual confession of the impossibility of transcribing the effect of the reality, except in an infinite and thus impossible text (Monet and Cézanne's obsessive work is in fact rather similar: they both continue to investigate the very same realities, the garden of Giverny and the Sainte Victoire). The description grasps, freezes the landscape and at the same time loses it:

> We passed the first great Promontory, & What a scene! Where I stand, on the shore is a triangular Bay, taking in the whole of the water view—on the other shore is a straight deep wall of Mist / & one third of the bare mountains stands out from behind it—the top of the wall only in the sun—the rest black–& now it is all one deep wall of white vapour, save that black streaks shaped like strange creatures, seem to move in it & down it, in opposite direction to the motion of the great Body!—& over the forks of the Cliff behind, in shape so like a cloud, the Sun sent cutting it his thousand silky Hairs of amber & green Light.[29]

A dash ("–") separates the previous scene from the following one: "I step two paces, and have lost the glory, but the edge has exactly the soft richness of the silver edge of a cloud behind which the Sun is travelling!"[30] The dash, the recurring graphic pause of Coleridge's prose, corresponds, on a territorial level, to the step of the walking poet: "I step". A surprising landscape, a completely *different* view, is the result of a small step, of a slight movement, which, however, changes everything from the scrap. Leaving behind the old patterns implies a complete freedom of movement, a constant change of perspective. It is no longer the conscience, but rather the body in its entirety (in the Nietzschean sense of the German word *Leib*) that prevails, the body and its logic, that of a somatic representation.

Coleridge discovers thus, thanks to the perspective of the moving body, a new source for the creation of landscapes. His attempt represents a radical aesthetic and an existential exercise of cultural

28. *Ibid.*, note 541.
29. *Ibid.*, note 551.
30. *Ibid*.

and permanent *decentralization*.³¹ He avoids the well ordered, geographical space in all of its aspects, psychological, phenomenological, social, etc., in order to create the condition of possibility for unfamiliar perceptions and, therefore, for the appearance of landscape. His very walks seem to have been imagined so that he can get lost³², to go as far as possible from the established reference systems (the poet defines himself justly as "an Inhabitant of another Planet³³"). Coleridge is never a "tourist of nature" (Maldiney). He prefers to experience the discontinuity, he is neither situated nor oriented but, through a powerful experience, a profane epiphany, he is able to experience an immediate fusion with what surrounds him. The experience in question is far from being mystical, on the contrary, it is absolutely concrete. Coleridge creates a void around himself, he learns to utterly renounce control as well as geographical, historical and cultural references. The poet's prose does not describe already-seen picturesque sites (it is not easy to read his *Notebooks*); it rather provides a constellation of elements that need to be connected to each other and thus surprises the reader. Coleridge's passages are always between the *placeable* and the *unplaceable* or, better: one can glimpse them in the intervals of his prose rather than in the stream of his words.

The eighteenth-century has been, and Coleridge confirms it, the century of a work on nature carried out primarily by the gaze. The next century will, conversely, be marked by the intervention of man in nature. The transformation on a vast scale of the European territory first, and of almost the entire surface of the earth in a second time, has been the indirect but fundamental cause of a further change concerning the perception of nature. The nineteenth-century was, in general, the century of the regulation, canalization and entrapment of the surviving 'natural' regions of the world. The rationalization of agriculture and forestry created new realities, while the growing industrialization modified the usual territorial structure and caused, at the same time, the first serious

---

31. See H.D. Baker, **Landscape as Textual Practise in Coleridge's Notebooks,** in **ELH,** 1992, 59, 3, 651-670.
32. See E. Straus, **Vom Sinn der Sinne,** Springer, Berlin 1956; H. Maldiney, *L'art,* *l'éclair de l'être,* 330; Id., *Ouvrir le rien. L'art nu,* 128 ss.
33. **The Notebooks of Samuel Taylor Coleridge,** note 551.

environmental problems.³⁴ The cultural landscape—the land that has pre-industrially been manipulated by man since the beginning of humanity—replaces now the nature that had been explored, conquered and catalogued during the previous century as a source of sublime or picturesque pleasures. The territorial laceration inflicted on nature by industrialization generates a radical dualism with the "good" old landscape—grown century after century—on the one hand, and the new non-places, products of a mechanical and technological civilization on the other.

The new interest in landscape—nature seemed, by then, already totally disenchanted, since it had been completely inscribed in the catalogue of images known to everyone—passes, once again, through a loss and a crisis. The German poet Annette von Droste-Hülshoff expresses this feeling as early as 1842:

> Such was the physiognomy of the country until now, and it will no longer be the same in forty years. Population and luxury grow quickly and together with them needs and industry. The small picturesque lands are going to be divided; the culture of the broadleaf forest that grows slowly is abandoned in order to leave space for coniferous forests which assure quick earnings. Soon fir trees and endless fields of grain will totally transform the character of the landscape and that of its inhabitants, who will forget their traditional habits and customs. Let us therefore sense and remember what is still here, before the shady blanket that is spreading all over Europe reaches this quiet corner of the earth.³⁵

Landscape is here unilaterally linked to the past. Hence, it takes the form of the idyll, of the romantic enclave which is based on the glorification of a reality that—in the fixity that is ascribed to it—has never really existed. This typical form of the landscape of the 19th century will have several consequences. It refers, firstly, to a static or eternal conception of the phenomenon: the good landscape will

---

34. See R.P. Sieferle, *Entstehung und Zerstörung der Landschaft*, in *Landschaft und Landschaften*, 238 ss; for France see J.-R. Pitte, *Histoire du paysage français*, Tallandier, Paris 2003.
35. A. von Droste-Hülshoff, *Bilder aus Westfalen*, in Id., *Werke*, Hanser, Munich 1970, 977.

be the untouched one, the one that will never change.[36] The need to protect it at any cost creates, at the same time, a political strategy of landscape. The latter will always forget the damaged territory, focusing its actions on the safeguard of everything that is traditional and already recognized. The blindness in front of a "violated nature"[37] and the ideological passion for the cultural landscape, by now confused with nature in general, work hand in hand. Such a nostalgic or romantic approach leads automatically to a conservative and traditionalist vision of landscape. Now, even the few surviving spots that somehow survived to the industrial civilization will have to coincide with the Arcadian imagination projected onto them.

The nineteenth-century offers thus a relief valve to the conscience, tired and saturated with picturesque and sublime effects, looking for nature as a human artifact rich in history. The intrinsic ambiguity of the glorification of nature refers though, ironically, to the conflict between man (as savior) and man (as builder-destroyer). The landscape genre, after having passed different crises and in need of a new motivation, will fully benefit from it: since nature can be discovered again and again (this time in search of the last idylls that resisted progress), the research carried out on site by the *plein air* painters will be able to appropriate the world as landscape once more.

The difference at work in Coleridge's attitude and notes had its origin in the subject. It concerned two rather distinct ways of approaching nature aesthetically: the experimental, anarchical one, exposed to risk and chance, and represented by the wandering poet; and the dominant one, deconstructed along the same path, in correspondence to the visual models of the time and culturally imposed. The difference which became visible thanks to the antagonism between new and old, organic and mechanical, fast and slow, small and large scale is of a peculiar kind. It refers to territoriality, that is to the object or the support of aesthetic appraisal. The territory of the majority of industrialized countries is, as we know, the object of conflicting attitudes. One attitude, calls for an unconditional attention to the historically-built landscape, while the other one

---

36. See M. Jakob, *Paysage et temps,* Infolio, Gollion 2007.

37. See P. Fedeli, *La natura violata. Ecologia e mondo romano,* Sellerio, Palermo 1990.

includes the idea of transformation and celebrates the "victory of work over nature[38]".

The first approach, characterized by the glorification of a certain type of landscapes, is still very much in use. It is forcedly based—as a fundamentally conservative and nostalgic attitude—on a policy of the image. The landscapes in question exist above all in the form of images, given that the perfection of the image does not expose any more the real site to time and change. This way of seeing nature as something to be protected requires a "freezing", an anesthesia of the idealized landscapes in order to distance them from any future evolution. Yet, this approach is not limited to the production or spreading of images; it rather imposes—in the name of a sentimental pseudo-archaeology—the adjustment of the reality to the image. This major trend has also played a central role in the constitution of various national landscapes.[39] The national landscape corresponds in fact, almost everywhere, to the old cultural or agricultural landscapes exposed—since the very moment of their definition as "national monuments"[40]—to the pressure of industrialization, rationalization and planning.[41]

The development of industry and tourism and the crisis of classical land management made landscape *enclaves* more and more precious. The landscape safeguard and protection movements—once the action of few critical voices like John Ruskin or a Ernst Rudorff—have come in quick succession until the present day. They are based, as proved by Paul Schultze-Naumburg's example (the German architect distinguished in his "Kulturarbeiten" the good, that is organic and old, versus most of the bad, or new architecture) on carefully selected and composed images that sense the essence of what has to be preserved at any cost. Most of the photographic campaigns

---

38. See V. Klemm, *Albrecht Daniel Thaer. Persönlichkeit und Werk*, in *DDR*, 27, 1978, 13-18.

39. See F. Cachin, *Le paysage du peintre*, in *Les lieux de mémoire*, t. II, *La nation*, ed.: P. Nora, Gallimard, Paris 1997, vol. I, *L'immatériel – Paysages*, 957-996 (transl*.: The Painter's Landscape* in *Rethinking France: Les Lieux de Mémoire, II: Space,* University of Chicago Press, Chicago 2006).

40. A. von Humboldt coined the term *Naturdenkmal*, Rudorff the term *Naturschutz* (1888).

41. The fight against the geometrization is a *Leitmotiv* in Rudorff's thought: "Due to the convenience of the straight line, the heights of the forests are razed to the ground" (*Über das Verhältnis des modernen Lebens zur Natur*, in Makowski, Buderath, *Die Natur*, 138).

30 Paul Cézanne, *Le découpage ferroviaire*, 1870-71

of the twentieth-century are still inscribed, independently of their specific reason, in an essentially conservative tradition. The perpetual perfection of the "frozen" landscape still dictates a policy based on iconic images like engravings, paintings, perspective drawings, postcards, posters, billboards, etc. Thanks to it, the fake or idealized landscape created by abstraction has become the true landscape, disremembering the main characteristic of nature, mutability. Such a postcard landscape does not demand attention, but faith, ideological adhesion. On a closer look, however, it only exists in the mind and in catalogues; hence the risk to disappoint us when we encounter the "real thing". The power and the appeal of this model ensue from the fact that it replaced the historical explanations. The desire to preserve the repertoire of "good landscapes" as such, to demand the subordination of the local reality to the bright image, is the expression of just another way to control nature rather than respecting it. The huge attention given to so-called "primeval" landscapes has its counterpart in the almost complete indifference towards the innumerable "violated" landscapes. Cézanne's *Découpage ferroviaire* (1870-71)—a canvas that shows the laceration inflicted on site during

31 Michelangelo Antonioni, *The Adventure* (*L'avventura*), final image

the construction of the railway—remains, from this point of view, an extraordinary document, in the strongest meaning of the term. A true awareness of an earth destroyed and polluted at large scale will take place only a century later in some important movies or in the work of the *"Land Artists"* of the late Sixties.

The works of Michelangelo Antonioni are among the very first in the history of cinema to systematically accord landscape a main role. His films cover the totality of nature, the sublime and violent one of an insular Mediterranean landscape, passing through the surprising effects of the urban landscape and the bewildering poetry of parks, up to the massively industrialized territories of the post-war period. Fascinated by the unusual aesthetic of industrial sites and landfills of any kind, Antonioni highlights what was previously excluded and visually censored, the "other" nature, modified, cut and reassembled until it became unrecognizable. The encounter with the outside world is always problematic in Antonioni's films, whether he shows the choc due to the experience of an unknown and hostile nature (*The Adventure*), the post-industrial non-places of Northern Italy (*Red Desert*) or an uncanny public space in *Blow-*

Up. Antonioni criticizes the tradition of postcard-landscapes (*L'Avventura*), the "eternal" and petrified image of a nature intended for tourism purposes[42], while featuring also the almost violent irruption of landscape as an aesthetic surprise (*Red Desert*).[43]

The artists gathered under the label of *Land Art* have given a whole new meaning to the venture "into" or "towards" nature, creating many of their installations in industrialized or heavily polluted places. Their attention, unlike the perspective of the neo-picturesque aesthetics of the *enclave*, is focused on the surprising attraction of deserted and dangerous places. Their paradoxical works do not hesitate to further transform nature thanks to the use of heavy vehicles—trucks and crawlers of any kind—employed in industry. They accept to be on the side of the artifice and indulge the presence of the "machine inside the garden" (of civilization). *Land Art* refers to landscape through a constant strategy of displacement and disorientation. Its probably most important effect in this field consists in the fact that it makes representation impossible: it dismantles the power of images. The artworks, exposed to the natural environment and no longer protected by the "auratic" sphere of the museum, denounce any attempt of documentation as abstract and forcedly insufficient ("The photographs betray the spirit of the work".[44] This kind of work of art thus exists only as a perpetual transformation—it participates in the time of nature—and demands an adequate reception: it is important to be patient, to walk around the site, to let oneself to be surprised and experience the impossibility of creating a compact image starting from a single point of view.

The relation between voluntary but exceptional stimulation (starting from the subject) and involuntary stimulation (starting from nature as an object that is at the same time destroyed and adulated)—an encounter that will once again transform the constitution of landscape—is partly the consequence of the new technologies of the nineteenth-century. Firstly, the construction of the railway system (the first train travelled in 1825, between Stockton and Darlington, in England)

---

42. See the last scene of *The Adventure*, which, starting from painting (Friedrich), questions the gaze on nature (exercised by the bourgeois subject).
43. See the famous final sequence of the *Eclipse*.
44. Thus wrote R. Smithson, *Incidents of Mirror-Travel in the Yucatan*, in *The Writings of Robert Smithson*, ed.: N. Holt, New York University Press, New York 1979, 94-95.

changed radically both what was still surviving as nature and the methods of its perception. Railways had an unprecedented impact on the territory. The linearity of the rails was seen as the action of a huge "knife"—the extended *hand* of civilization—that eviscerated the earth.[45] The train created both a spatial network consisting of fixed points, and a temporal network, characterized by regulated time. The territory, for the first time, was no longer defined starting from the human perspective, but it followed the cold, rational one of the machine. Since the development of the railway system, we have been living—and this is even truer nowadays—in territories designed and modified by technology. The construction of the rail network required at the same time, especially in Europe, massive interventions: the creation of countless viaducts, bridges, tunnels, embankments, etc. The national or characteristic landscape, the landscape-image destined to become "eternal", was necessarily touched by the phenomenon, given its widespread dissemination[46] and the desire to take the tourists to the places catalogued by the tourism industry. The precious reserves, the landscapes worshipped by conservation at any price risked, all of a sudden, to pay the price of the ongoing transformation of the surface of the earth. This anxiety was expressed by one of the most eminent proponents of landscape protection, John Ruskin:

> You have despised nature; that is to say, all the deep and sacred sensations of natural scenery. The French revolutionists made stables of the cathedrals of France; you have made racecourses of the cathedrals of the earth. Your one conception of pleasure is to drive in railroad carriages round their aisles, and eat off their altars. You have put a railroad bridge over the fall of Schaffhausen. You have tunneled the cliffs of Lucerne by Tell's chapel; you have destroyed the Clarens shore of the Lake of Geneva; there is not a quiet valley in England that you have not filled with bellowing fire.[47]

45. See, in this regard, Zola's remarkable novel *La Bête humaine* (*The Beast Within*); see also G. Schivelbusch, *Geschichte der Eisenbahnreise. Zur Industrialisierung von Raum und Zeit im 19. Jahrhundert*, Fischer, Frankfurt am Main 2000 (transl.: *The railway journey: the industrialization of time and space in the 19th Century,* The University of California Press, Los Angeles 1986).

46. It is, actually, a more complex system, designed by Desportes as a "metal-steam-coal system" (see M. Desportes, *Paysages en mouvement. Transports et perception de l'espace XVIIIe -XXe siècle,* Gallimard, Paris 2005, 99-100).

47. J. Ruskin, *Sesame and Lilies,* George Allen, London 1895, 132.

32 *IRT Ninth Avenue Line*, New York, around 1896

The dualism at the basis of the policy of the landscape as a perfect image was therefore threatened by the intrusion of the enemy—the train, later the automobile—in the aesthetic *enclaves*. It was a policy that suffered also from a greater pressure, exercised by the hidden or forgotten realities revealed by the railway. The rail system, in fact, did not cease to show the concealed face of the world: the yard of the buildings, the neglected areas in close proximity to the stations, the newly transformed places, etc.

> From the train, passengers see the rear views of a place. They view not main roads or city street, not town walls or central squares or prominent facades, but rather the back sides of factories, warehouses, workers' quarters, and older structures rudely served by the development of the railroad. Rail travelers thus peer at places perhaps never meant to be displayed or observed, and certainly not designed for the train's rolling and rushing manner of perception.[48]

48. M. Schwarzer, *Zoomscape. Architecture in Motion and Media*, Princeton Architectural Press, New York 2004, 59.

The modern transport system itself as an hyper-visible reality (its development was accompanied, from the beginning, by a marketing campaign able to exploit emblematic images) and the new technological landscape that it created caused an increasingly vigorous reaction from those who, by then, could find countless reasons to preserve the landscape heritage. The conservative position that demanded the perpetuity of landscape (the tiny spots worthy of being protected) was furthermore destabilized by a another factor linked to the development of transport technology: the new perception of the world given from a moving point of view. The first reaction in front of images that flew too rapidly was shock. The American writer Nathaniel Hawthorne described this situation accurately in the 1850s:

> At one moment, they were rattling through a solitude; the next, a village had grown up around them; a few breaths more and it had vanished, as if swallowed by an earthquake [...] Everything was unfixed from its age-long rest, and moving at whirlwind speed in a direction opposite to their own.[49]

The train journey caused dizziness, and it needed an effort of the eye in order to learn to control the speed and the impressions. Seen from the moving vehicle, everything became unusual: the perspective was both surprisingly vast, panoramic, and an inebriating flux:

> The scene behind the carriage window-panes / Goes flitting past in furious flight; whose plains / With streams and harvest-fields and trees and blue / Are swallowed by the whirlpool, where into / The telegraph's slim pillars topple o'er, / Whose wires look strangely like a music-score.[50]

The regularity of the movement provided a persistent temporal rhythm to the visual perception, while the windows, offering an oblique view, framed the outside world in an unusual manner.

The perspective from the vehicle in motion links the continuity of the journey to the discontinuity of the rapidly following percep-

---

49. N. Hawthorne, *The House of the Seven Gables*, in *The Complete Novels and Selected Tales of Nathaniel Hawthorne*, Random House, New York 1937, 397.

50. P. Verlaine, *La bonne chanson* VII (1870); transl.: *The scene behind the carriage window-panes* in *Poems of Paul Verlaine*, Duffield and Co., New York 1906.

tions. The diagonal view offered composite images that no longer correspond to the spatial sequence of traditional perspective levels: the foreground completely disappears in the fluctuating flow of impressions, while the background seems strangely unlimited. It presents unknown and unusual content, including that related to technological infrastructures. The discomfort caused by speed prevents, at first, any visual relation with the outside and the production of stable images. At the beginning, travelers did not identify landscapes; they were rather the spectators of a surprising flow of impressions, impossible to fix at any given moment. However, the effect of dissociation and dizziness represented only one aspect of this new experience of the world. The other one is characterized by a new sense of unity as the sum of various discontinuities. Privileging the discursive structure of the rapid images, the train perspective gave in other words birth to unusual sequences and series, in short, it anticipated clearly the "images in movement" to come in films.[51]

The new kinetic aesthetic is opposed to the motionless image specific to the pre-impressionist artistic tradition that is at the basis of the immobile landscape promoted by its nostalgic enthusiasts. Until the advent of the modern infrastructures, the viewer projected in certain circumstances his gaze towards nature and created a landscape or a series of landscapes. Now, instead, the image of nature unfolds before his eyes spontaneously, and it is the technological point of view that sets the perspective; it is the speed of the accelerated vehicle, and no longer the human movement, that dictates the structure and the quality of the visual impressions. In his carriage, the traveler of the eighteenth-century could see and cross nature at the same time. On the train, for the modern traveler nature is reduced to a fiction, an appealing and fleeing exteriority. With the rail system, nature is definitively kept at distance.[52] The view from the train thus generates a series of meta-landscapes, unstable and disconcerting landscape-films of sorts. The view from the automo-

---

51. See L. Kirby, *Parallel Tracks: The Railroad and Silent Cinema*, Duke University Press, Durham 1997.
52. The next stage will be reached not by the automobile—relatively *freer* than the train—but by the television. The latter represents the triumph of the immobility of the subject, who makes the totality of the images of the world come to him.

bile[53], on the other hand, recovers frontality and creates, unlike the railway perspective, the powerful illusion of an individual, narcissistic control of the visual space (more akin to the traditional way of organizing visual perception). The American artist Tony Smith talks about his astonishment in 1950, after the rediscovery of the world seen from the car:

> The drive was a revealing experience. The road and much of the landscape was artificial, and yet it couldn't be called a work of art. On the other hand, it did something for me that art had never done. At first I didn't know what it was, but its effect was to liberate me from many of the views I had had about art. It seemed that there had been a reality there which had not had any expression in art. The experience on the road was something mapped out but not socially recognized. I thought to myself, it ought to be clear that's the end of art [...] There is no way you can frame it, you just have to experience it.[54]

The aesthetic of the automobile shares with that of the railway the landscape-as-a-film, the metamorphic sequence of images that succeed endlessly one after the other.[55] It also causes, thanks to its greater freedom of movement, dazzling encounters, unique and ephemeral. The chance of being surprised, as Coleridge's experience suggests, is fulfilled in the twentieth-century, paradoxically, thanks to modern technology. Its artificial perspective generates—in a standardized universe devoid of mystery—powerful and unexpected aesthetic sensations, impossible to frame ("There is no possibility of framing all of this"). The landscape-film[56] represents potentially a lethal thorn at the heart of the neo-pictorial aesthetic of immobility and idyll.

The anachronistic blindness of a conservation policy of landscape that aims at beautiful enchanted reserves—the *landscape-as-postcard* ideology—becomes immediately visible when con-

---

53. See D. Appleyard, K. Lynch, J.R. Myers, *The View from the Road*, MIT Press, Cambridge, Mass. 1964; S. Giedion, *Space, Time, and Architecture*, MIT Press, Cambridge, Mass. 1967, 826-832. For the difference between railway/automobile, see Schivelbusch. *Geschichte*, 41.
54. T. Smith, *Talking with Tony Smith*, in *Artforum*, December 1966, 5, 19.
55. See Virginia Woolf's *Orlando* and *Mrs Dalloway*; see Schwarzer. *Zoomscape*, 96 ss.

fronted to the aesthetics of the unstable, of the ephemeral and of the temporal processes made possible by modern locomotion technologies of the nineteenth- and twentieth-century. The new *techno-kinetic* gaze has successfully absorbed the tradition of the postcard-image. In fact, the train allowed to approach (almost pedagogically) not only selected natural sceneries, but it also was at the origin of the creation of new landscapes:

> Already during the 1850s in the United States, books were published consisting of stereoscopic and photographic views of dramatic scenes along rail lines. In the 1870s, travel guides commissioned photographers and painters to illustrate choice vistas along the Western lines. The landscapes popularized by railroads encompassed mountain ranges and river gorges, as well as the elements of the rail corridor itself, including bridges, tunnels, stations, and the infinite miles of track and the telegraph wire.[57]

The automobile marked a further stage in this development. The initial transgressive quality of the mobile perspective weakened and eventually disappeared; the "view from the road" (Appleyard/ Lynch) became indeed the instrument that permitted to control the world "outside", with the consequence of completely integrating whatever was left over as a "natural" form in the roadway system. It is, however, on a territorial level that the repercussion, from the point of view of the automobile, has been particularly effective. From the end of the second World War onwards, the perspective of the driver in his car gives has modeled everywhere the shape of the earth. The alteration of the world is not limited to the creation of a tentacular network of streets, garages, service stations, car parks, etc. It also touches the re-designed cities and urban landscapes[58], the suburbs and intermediate spaces, developed at a rapid pace. Only a small step separates the appeal that comes from the automotive perspective expressed by Sigfried Giedion ("The space-time feeling of our period can seldom be felt so keenly as when driving, the wheel under one's hands, up and down hills, beneath overpasses, up ramps and over giant bridges"[59])

56. See G. Bruno, *Driven*, in *Inside Cars*, ed.: J. Abbott Miller, Princeton University Press, Princeton 2001.
57. Schwarzer, *Zoomscape*, 58.
58. See G. Cullen, *Townscape,* The Architectural Press, London 1961.
59. Schwarzer, *Zoomscape*, 77.

from *Autopia*, the absolute supremacy of the car giving form to a world made by concrete and asphalt, an *Asphalt Earth*.

The elusive today

By definition, any attempt to situate the present in which we live appears highly problematic given our lack of historical distance. The interpretation of the current condition will almost always coincide with the recent situation projected in a *tomorrow* with an uncertain outline.These final observations will start once again from the concept of representation. Throughout our study two forms of landscape have been identified: the pictorial representation, the only one, during long centuries, designated as *landscape*, and the empirical or mental representation, which is relatively recent. The first one is a form of manifestation[60], a vision of nature *through* the image; actually, in this case nature is never truly present and it remains at a distance, feared and absent. The history of this landscape-image has been outlined briefly (see *supra*, Ch. IV).

The second form corresponds to the possibility of visualizing a piece of nature as an image on site. In this case we are confronted with an "awareness of a presence, an experience of the reality of an object [here: landscape] that co-exists with myself here and now, and determines my mood".[61] Here something becomes visible as such, without any previous mediation provided through prior models.

This later variant, which implies the encounter between a subject and nature, is however not necessarily a pure or simple appearance either. The surprise and the immediacy connected with the landscape experience, the fact that the landscape seems to "respond" directly to our sensitivity, should not obscure the peculiarity of a human perception that has always been structured and organized. It is up to the discursive logic of the perceptual mechanism to facilitate, if not to make possible, the identification of what is worthy of catching our attention, and this according both to individual preferences and to the general approach privileged by a given period or culture. Landscape thus does not refer to the image only in its first variant, but in the second case as well, where a selection, or better, an attention of the subject, stems from the knowledge of other,

---

60. B. Waldenfels, in *Was ist ein Bild?*, ed.: G. Boehm, Fink, Munich 1994, 234.

61. H. Jonas, in *Ibid.*, 116.

33 *Oceandome*, Miyazaki, Japan, 2002

previously known images (especially those of the landscape genre). As soon as the two phenomena begin to exist in parallel, from the eighteenth-century onwards, things become more complicated. The real problems, however, will arise in the second half of the twentieth-century, a period that is not only thirsty for images but that also is, as Hans-Georg Gadamer formlated, *reproduktionssüchtig*[62], obsessed with unbounded reproduction.

To talk about the primacy and the ubiquitous presence of the image today does not imply a purely iconic processes. The initial phase of the pictorial landscape already obeyed, as we know, a precise rhetoric. In the rare cases when human figures were missing from the paintings—or better, where the narration seemed unclear—there was "nothing to see", as the critics of the time highlighted, and no aesthetic pleasure to gain. The landscape-images are inscribed in a rhetorical-narrative system, and it is always the narrative that provides the meaning and *raison d'être* of the natural elements represented in the painting. The essential role of the association of ideas, comparisons and other patterns already mentioned shows that the empirical experience of landscape corresponds rather to a "reading" than to a mere casual encounter due to a sudden appearance. The modern status of the image is not devoid of deep repercussions on the landscape, and this is not a surprise, given the intimacy of both phenomena.

Our time has not only known the exponential growth of the images that circulate throughout the world: it continues to multiply and discover new mediums that generate families of new images. *Advertising-images*, *television-images*, *digital-images* are shown on the giant screens of *media-buildings* and take a more private shape on the displays of mobile phones, permeating the totality of cultural forms. Our everyday life is directly touched by these modifications, to the point that it contributes to the development of a subject whose identity is created through images, an "image-self" or a "fractal-self", in Jean Baudrillard's words. The traditional photo albums have been replaced by personal videos, web pages, blogs, or avatars. Real life is always somewhere else, where the image is, ephemeral but exposed and accessible to the others. Life now imitates the image; the

---

62. *Was ist ein Bild?*, 90.

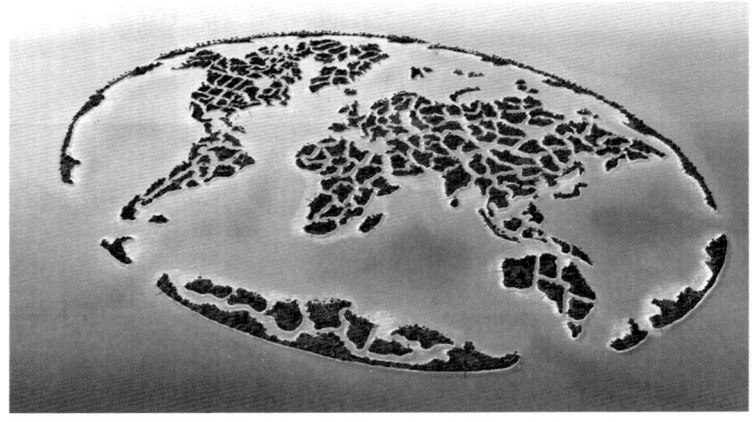

34 *The World*, Dubai, 2007

postmodern subject aspires to appear perfectly in it, and not only during the big events in which everything is arranged in order to result in beautiful images (birth, wedding, holidays), but on every occasion, given the omni-presence of the electronic eyes that spy on us, without interruption.

The image, object of a ubiquitous fascination, thus drags the reality, integrates it and even utterly transforms it. The feeling of being, always and everywhere, surrounded by images—produced by ourselves or imposed by society or by others—reminds one of a situation that is evoked in the most famous Platonic myth: that of the cave, where men see apparitions and shadows and take them for reality, having no other way to access it, clouded as they are by their illusions. We too have learnt to confuse images and reality; this confusion contributes to the development of ways of life characterized by stasis and voluntary self-alienation: by now, the whole world comes to us or towards us *as* image, and everyone absorbs, so to speak, the reality at will. The *being-in-the-world* has been replaced by the *being-in-the-images*, in an undefinable "somewhere". We gladly take part in this disorientation of the image as long as the spectacle continues. The *Ocean Dome*, an exotic artificial beach built at the end of the 20th century in Miyazaki, Japan, only 300 meters from a real beach, perfectly symbolizes this development. The image of the beach and that of the eternally blue sky replace the authenticity through a spectacle-reality. The landscape on the background and the sky do not promise anything anymore; they, as images, guarantee the fiction of the huge commercial simulacrum that allows, symbolically, to avoid any movement and the exposure to the vicissitudes of existence (time, meteorology, seasons). The replacement of the world with its image finds another powerful expression in a project in Dubai. While the artificial island that depicts a giant palm (*The Palm*) replaces a plant, swallowing everything in its dominant structural form, the (abandoned) urban project *The World* goes much further: it represents, as an inhabited image, the world in its totality, concentrating it in one single site accessible to the *happy few*.

Today, everything that is not worthy of becoming an image seems already obsolete, non-existent. Hence, a form of permanent distraction due to the incessant zapping and to the impossibility of facing the totality of the images produced. The cultural filter imposed by images (the ones that have a major visibility) operates thus a clear selection.

The second aspect of the current predominance of the image is characterized by the multiplication of points of view. We are about to undergo, perhaps without even realizing it, a cultural revolution. The central perspective that has dominated Western history from Brunelleschi to the advent of the television (a technology and an ideology that, over the centuries, has been imposed to the whole world) must now share its absolute position with other, that is multiple perspectives. The static anthropic perspective, which permitted the visual control of the world, has been surpassed by the post-human one of the machine, namely the satellites. *Google Earth* and the geographic information systems (based on former military programs) are not only providing surprising views of the earth's surface, they also dictate—as shown by the example of Dubai—contemporary land management. The eyes of satellites and surveillance cameras destabilize the human gaze: anthropomorphism turns into technomorphism.

Of course the automobile already imposed, in part, its vision and marked the world via architecture and land management. In 1967, Guy Debord wrote: "The dictatorship of the automobile—the pilot product of the first stage of commodity abundance—has left its mark on the landscape with the dominance of freeways, which tear up the old urban centers and promote an ever wider dispersal"[63]. The outlook of the world from the automobile shakes the frontal logic, structured and static, for the benefit of a more panoramic, vast and "nervous" view.

The knowledge of a traditional world, built by the *homo erectus* from the data found in front of him and embodied by central perspective, changes with the new means of locomotion. The satellite, dragging extraterritorial elements devoid of human presence, imposes its point of view by weakening the traditional frontal gaze. It re-territorializes the vision of the world providing unusual images whose aesthetics has repercussions on today's practices of representation. Yann-Arthus Bertrand's photographic tours (the "elevation" of the photographic point of view characterizes in reality the entire 20th century), dedicated to the earth seen from the sky, adopt an elevated point of view at the expense of the apparently obsolete, more classical perspectives. The "beauty" of the earth as it appears from the distance creates a new geography, a graphic impression of the world. It implies, starting from the surprising images of the photographer-aviator-prophet, the denial of the terrestrial and somatic perspective of the walking subject who stops in front of something he wants to grasp with his gaze.

The worldwide success of the exhibition of such photographs indicates the extraordinary appeal of the recent "cosmic" perspective. Displaying these photographs outdoors, turning them into a spectacle that cancels everything that surrounds the photographic show, corresponds to the same logic that inspires *The World* project in Dubai: that of the replacement or the concentration of the world *in* the image. The new technical possibilities shift all the attention from reality towards its representation. The reality of the world catalogue of monuments and landscapes preserved by the UNESCO, for

---

63. G. Debord, *La société de spectacle,* Gallimard, Paris 1996, 168 (transl.: *The society of the spectacle,* Zone Books, New York 1995).

example, is no longer truly associated to the respective geographic sites, but rather to Internet sites; in short, it is digital. The identity of a project of landscape management or architecture is, too, increasingly anchored to the image: the self-referential project is developed on the screen and goes through virtual phases of digital visualization. Once the project is realized, its monitoring will be conducted thanks to digital photographic or filmic procedures; its assessment, the identification of its social or cultural value, will also imply the image. Real life is again always *elsewhere*, in the visual data, to the point that the perspective provided by webcams seems more real than the filmed subject itself. Modern architecture and landscape architecture gladly submit themselves to this tendency, for example recommending the elaboration of projects that start from the logo—the image par excellence—of the future realization: "Design theorist Robert Somol has suggested, with regard to the architecture of OMA, that shape operates with *the graphic immediacy of the logo*. One can indeed speculate, with mixed feelings, on a transition from strong figures (nineteenth century) to irregular shapes (twentieth century) to parks as logos (twenty-first century)".[64]

The recent tendency of contemporary art, which privileges photography, goes in the same direction. The large formats (overmodernity generates overformats) of Gursky, Wall, Linke, Hütte, Burckhardt, and so on, with their extraordinary reproduction quality, seem to indicate that today the true encounter with reality happens necessarily through the image. The knowledge of the world coincides therefore, now more than ever, with the knowledge of its iconic mark. Photographic hyperrealism appears thus as a logical consequence of the control that the image exercises over the world. If, in the Netherlands of the seventeenth-century, painting used to react to the threat of new technologies—represented by the telescope and the microscope—proposing an extreme descriptive realism[65], contemporary artistic photography reacts to the loss of reality offering increasingly clear images. By doing so, however, it contributes to reinforce even more the dictatorship exercised by images. Reality

---

64. J. Czerniak, *Introduction/Speculating on Size*, in *Large Parks*, ed.: J. Czerniak and G. Hargreaves, Princeton Architectural Press, New York 2007, 26.

65. See S. Alpers, *The Art of Describing*, The University of Chicago Press, Chicago 1983.

35 *Former industrial site*, landscape architect Peter Latz, Turin, Italy

is nowadays under pressure, it weakens, while the image triumphs. Living inside the iconic-digital palimpsest also presumes, however, the strong return of the verbal sphere, of standardized words in accordance with the images themselves. In the age of universal circulation of images, everything has already been seen and read, everything refers to something we have already seen or heard of; with the consequence that the landscapes of the world resemble each other more and more, instead of differentiating themselves and surprising us.

CHAPTER VI

PROBLEMS AND FUTURE PERSPECTIVES

As an aesthetic phenomenon and a historic object, landscape will never be explained in an exhaustive manner. To thematize it means to to delimit its different qualities, in the hope of bringing to light a large part of its infinite facets.

The majority of landscape theories privilege a philosophical point of view. Landscape is seen as intimately connected to subjectivity. Such a post-idealistic position is fully inscribed in a discourse that, in almost two centuries, has never ceased to speak about the subject while affronting the landscape. Besides, the supreme point of view that characterizes philosophical elevation is well matched with the elevated point of view favorable to the constitution of landscape. The eidetic superiority and the visual supremacy are related to the same ideology, which, in general, forgets or sets aside non-philosophical constitutive factors.

Over the last decades, several English speaking researchers have emphasized the social constitution of the landscape phenomenon.[1] Another forgotten but important aspect is however represented by technology; there exists a series of artifacts, invented and developed over the centuries, that have contributed, directly or indirectly, to the constitution of landscape. The history of the relation between technology and landscape is still in great part to be reconstructed and to be written. It begins, arguably, with the activity of the hand of man, the first technical instrument, which leaves traces on the territory.[2]

> Human activities become inscribed within a landscape such that every cliff, large tree, stream, swampy area becomes a familiar place. Daily passages through the landscape become biographic encounters for individuals, recalling traces of past activities and previous events [...] All locales and landscapes are therefore embedded in the social and individual times of history.[3]

The act of walking is related to that of writing, it inscribes human traces in the territory:

---

1. See Cosgrove, *Social Formation and Symbolic Landscape*, x ss.; Mitchell, *Landscape and Power*, 1-34.

2. Tilley, *A Phenomenology of Landscape*, 27, 29-30.

3. *Ibid.*, 27.

36 Hieronymus Rodler, *Ein schön nützlich büchlein...* (1531)

If writing solidifies or objectifies speech into a material medium, a text, which can be read and interpreted, an analogy can be drawn between a pedestrian speech act and its inscription or writing on the ground in the form of the path or track. Both are sedimented traces of activity, and both provide ways to be followed. A strong path is inscribed through a forest or across a tract of heathland through a multitude of pedestrian speech acts that keep it open; a strong text is also one that is kept open, read many times.[4]

When retracing the history of technology in a broad sense, it is necessary to emphasize the contribution of the landscape frescoes in ancient Roman villas. The legendary *skené* of antique drama, the mobile background, whose invention, according to Vitruvius, is attributable

4. *Ibid.*, 30.

to Agatarcus[5], turns into mural painting, a form of representation that functions already as the "open window" celebrated in the Renaissance by Leon Battista Alberti. The mural depiction of the most varied landscapes (see *supra*, Ch. IV) anticipates the use of the window as a framing device.

> The act of opening a window is the founding act of a painting. When a painter opens a window onto the surface it's not like when, in the morning, he opens his eyes; it is rather as if a deity has opened his eyes in order to create the morning. This first act of the painter, the immense act of the eye that opens, consists in a totally material act: simply drawing a square on a wall. […] In order for a landscape to exist, there has to be distance. The window is the instrument that creates this distance.[6]

The shape of the window has been, since then, the common denominator of a multitude of instruments that allow to focus visual reality in the most efficient way. The famous perspective built and exhibited in 1425, in Florence, by Brunelleschi, the grid (velo, reticolato) described and used by Alberti, Leonardo and Dürer all work as practical machines that organize a new vison of the world, technical tools that, at the same time, have a huge impact on painting and, consequently, on the landscape genre.

> An image built starting from one-point perspective can be interpreted independently of its meaning, by deciding (and until that moment it would have been nonsensical) whether the represented thing is shown *as it is in the reality* or not: the representation method does no longer refer to readability (readable/unreadable dichotomy) or interpretation, but it belongs, from the philosophical point of view, to the category of quality, given that the image presents itself as a spatial fact.[7]

The countless *belvederes* found in gardens (terraces, loggias, towers, galleries, artificial hills, etc.), as architectural devices built with pre-

---

5. See Marco Vitruvio Pollione, *De architectura*, 329 (VII, 5).
6. G. Wajcman, *Fenêtre. Chroniques du regard et de l'intime*, Verdier, Paris 2004, 89, 233-234, 253.
7. Schmeiser, *Die Erfindung der Zentralperspektive*, 43.

37 Odilon Redon, *L'oeil, comme un ballon bizarre se dirige vers l'infini* (1882)

cision, create controllable images transposable into the aesthetical field. Technology, however, does not just constitute fascinating and static visions. While the effect of visual dizziness induced by the telescope is mainly due to the freedom of the hand that directs it, the *Claude Glass* allows to filter reality, always starting from a hand-eye relationship, in order to create at will landscapes that result from the encounter between chance and necessity, freedom and constraint.

> Gilpin, pursuing his reflections on the convex mirror, its ability to bring together various objects in one glance and to ground the composition, states that the eye is unable to examine simultaneously the "general effects"—"nature at large"…(composition)—and "particular objects". On the other hand, the convex mirror brings "composition, forms and colours" closer together. Thus the Claude mirror, a reductive instrument, is a supplement to vision; but as Jacques Derrida has shown, the notion of supplement has two indissociable meanings. In the first, the mirror is a surplus: coupled with sight, it constitutes an increase by adding a plenitude to another plenitude. The black mirror emerges as a supplement of painting and is enriched by this cumulative function. But it also supplants. In this sense, the mirror is less an addition than a replacement: it is put "in the place of"; it fills a void.[8] The controlled movement of the hand is replaced, later on, by the dynamic energy of modern vehicles (the train, the automobile, the plane, which all influence our perception, described by Schivelbusch, Schwarzer or Desportes[9]).

The impact of these technical objects, connected to the idea of control and to the possibility of addressing the eye, has shaped the history of landscape. Their influence is not limited to one-point perspective; it equally affects the perspective of the travelers and of socio-cultural patterns projected on the beautiful, sublime or picturesque nature.

Each one of these elements would allow—and even request—the re-writing of the history of landscape, for example starting with the

8. A. Maillet, *The Claude Glass. Use and Meaning of the Black Mirror in Western Art*, Zone Books, New York 2004, 96, 100-101.

9. Schivelbusch, *Geschichte der Eisenbahnreise;* Schwarzer, *Zoomscape*; Desportes, *Paysages en mouvement*.

impact that the first hot-air balloon (1783) had on landscape consciousness, with the success of panoramas as a substitute for 'real' landscapes, or with the initial shock experimented by the early train travelers terrified and at the same time fascinated by what they saw.

> "Annihilation of space and time" was the early-nineteenth-century characterization of the effect of railroad travel [...] and the train was described as a projectile [...] The train was experienced as a projectile, and traveling on it, as being shot through the landscape—thus losing control of one's senses. "In travelling on most of the railways...", says an anonymous author of the year 1844, "the face of nature, the beautiful prospects of hill and dale, are lost or distorted to our view." [...] We have seen how the nineteenth-century travelers gradually got accustomed to what at first seemed frightening: the demolition of traditional space-time relationships and the dissolution of reality. The travelers developed new modes of behavior and perceptions, forms in which the new experimental content included itself.[10]

The history of these technologies complicates and undermines the traditional reconstructions of landscape, asks for substantial digressions. At the same time, it sheds light on a more ambiguous and dialectic development: the window has worked, of course, as an object that opened onto the world, but it also acted as an instrument of dispossession and control (the exclusive point of view of a prince); the method of one-point perspective, as it has been taught and divulged over the centuries, remains an exclusive instrument, within the reach of the educated eye; the panorama, the fascinating panscopic device that let people 'travel' to places they would never have visited, represents at the same time a perverse substitute remedy.

The history of nineteenth-century visual perception, admirably narrated by Jonathan Crary in *Techniques of the Observer* [11], reveals, too, the fundamental ambiguities inherent to the field of landscape. It would therefore be necessary to analyze the landscape taking into account the impact of modern perceptive machines (satellites, surveillance cameras, webcams, scanners, digital recording devices, etc.).

---

10. Schivelbusch, *Geschichte der Eisenbahnreise*, 52, 53, 143.

11. J. Crary, *Techniques of the Observer*, MIT Press, Cambridge Mass. 1990.

The term urban landscape and its recent success[12] are not less problematic. Historically and theoretically, landscape has always been the *other* of the city, according to the double meaning of this formula, that is the *non-city*, but also something that—precisely as *its* other—interests and exists only thanks to the gaze exercised by the city itself. It is thus essential, especially in the field of human sciences, not to confuse and dilute such concepts; any rushed generalization will reduce their operative power for the benefit of undifferentiated and vague statements. It is worth mentioning the historical dialectic of the city and the non-city (country, landscape) in its most varied forms, from the Hellenistic period to the advent of mass landscape tourism organized by and for the citizens. Equally, the different temporalities of city and landscape should be taken into account: the first one, urban space, is completely marked by the rhythm of human activities[13]; the latter, landscape, is characterized both by the intervention of man on the territory and by the time of nature. Certainly, nature has been able to penetrate the city across the centuries in the form of gardens, parks, squares, avenues, etc. In the city, however, nature remains heteronomous because of the immediate presence of the urban, constructed element and the control that it exercises, while landscape evokes the ideas of independence and freedom. "Letting nature into the city does by no means imply that the feeling of alienation towards nature has been overcome; simply, the man-nature relationship changes from *relationship with the outside* to *extrinsic relationship*".[14] This fundamental difference has visual consequences as well. Landscape, as it has already been highlighted, is inseparable from an open spatiality, characterized for instance by the idea of the horizon.[15] The structured universe that characterizes the urban space on the other hand is walled-up; seen from this point of view, landscape will appear as what exists "outside", providing the possibility to transcend the closed visual system of the urban environment and the constructed elements that hide the horizon.

12. The first occurrence of "urban landscape" is found in Rodenbach's *Bruges-la-Morte* (1892).
13. See Assunto, *Il paesaggio e l'estetica*, 65 ss. and 114 ss.
14. G. Böhme, *Für eine ökologische Naturästhetik*, Suhrkamp, Frankfurt am Main 1989, 64.
15. See M. Collot, *L'horizon fabuleux*, José Corti, Paris 1988; A. Koschorke, *Die Geschichte des Horizonts. Grenze und Grenzüberschreitung* in *literarischen Landschaftsbildern*, Suhrkamp, Frankfurt am Main 1990.

Besides, wishing to identify city and landscape too quickly implies a problem of comparability. The city is, by definition, complex, dense, layered; it stretches and is erected on a territory that is different from that of the landscape.[16] The success of the concept of urban landscape is also manifest in a literary trend that could be identified as new territorial writing or psycho-geographic prose. The fact that recent literature, in search of paradoxical impressions, looks towards the city, and especially suburbs, empty spaces or uncultivated lands, is worthy of attention. Iain Sinclair, Jean Rolin, Philippe Vasset or François Bon's works follow in the footsteps of a point of view that reveals the city as a sort of hyper-landscape: "On my part, for a long time, I have been searching for the point of view that would *reveal* the city".[17] They all seem attracted by the marginal sphere of waste and insignificant remains, and try to decipher an ordinary reality made up of graffiti, anonymous inscriptions, and mute architectures: "I found nothing but perfectly ordinary things (rubbish, wrecks of automobiles, washing machines) or, on the contrary, absolutely indefinable things (ditches and hills whose exact purpose remains a mystery; ruins that are too destroyed or too unclear to be identified; plates of concrete that rise from the ground, etc.)"[18] These authors collect, as if they were garbage-men of the gaze, the confused chaos of a postmodern urban universe where there is nothing to fix and where real (meteorological) time has disappeared.[19] Here, things are mostly standardized, repetitive, as François Bon notices: "Shopping area between the canal, the street and the rails, a garage, Monsieur Meuble's furniture factory, a DIY shop and another with a huge sign that says only Gardening, inevitable also the typical and standardized Buffalo Grill"[20]. During the almost psychotic strolls[21] of these lonely urban *wolves*, the peri-urban territory sometimes becomes a landscape, though only where it presents itself in its dehumanized

---

16. This is a state of things that certainly became more complicated from the moment when the created landscapes began to look more and more like *topoi*. In light of an increasing urbanization and a destructuring of the territory during the twentieth century, as well as the widespread city, the urban versus non-urban difference risks becoming progressively thin, or disappearing.

17. P. Vasset, *Un livre blanc*, Fayard, Paris 1995, 85.
18. *Ibid.*, 98.
19. "There's no weather here" (I. Sinclair, *Lights out for the Territory*, Granta, London 1997, 89).
20. F. Bon, *Paysage fer*, Verdier, Paris 2000, 13 and 12.
21. "The paranoia of travel is delightful" (Sinclair, *Lights out*, 44).

and dead form, where the city unfolds as a huge, fascinating, yet inanimate spectacle. It is as if in the chipped and unlivable territory of over-modernity, nature had reclaimed again its rights, transforming thus the urban sphere into a huge ruin.

The increasing attention given to the urban and peri-urban territory, including its most unexpected aspects (the surprising effects of dirt, of chaos and urban sadness), is also present in contemporary landscape architecture, which, over the last few decades, is more and more oriented towards the city and its malfunctions. The most avant-garde landscape architecture has become often a therapeutic instrument: it fixes the countless 'wounds' in the urban environment, the abandoned places of unclear purpose (old storages, factories, landfills, military bases, etc.), and invents new spaces, more suitable for a life form exposed to industrial decline.[22] Landscape urbanism, an important new discipline, has further highlighted the unique capacity of landscape architecture. The knowledge of ecology in general and of living processes in particular, as well as the skill to design on the long term make landscape architecture a far more efficient practice than the traditional disciplines of planning, and especially classical urbanism with its rigid and upside-down point of view.

> Landscape is a Medium, uniquely capable of responding to temporal change, transformation, adaptation, and succession. These qualities recommend landscape as an analog to contemporary processes of urbanization and as a medium uniquely suited to the open-endedness, indeterminacy, and change demanded by contemporary urban conditions [...] As such, landscape urbanism offers an implicit critique of architecture and urban's design inability to offer coherent, competent, and convincing explanations of contemporary urban conditions. In this context, the discourse surrounding landscape urbanism can be read as a disciplinary realignment in which landscape urbanism supplants architecture's historical role as the basic building block of urban design.[23]

---

22. See E.K. Meyer, *Uncertain Parks: Disturbed Sites, Citizens, and Risk Society*, in *Large Parks*, ed.: J. Czerniak, G. Hargreaves, Princeton Architectural Press, New York 2007, 59-86.

23. C. Waldheim, *Landscape as Urbanism*, in Id., *The Landscape Urbanism Reader*, Princeton Architectural Press, New York 2005, 39 and 37.

38 *Beautiful bodies in the industrail waste land*, Vogue 2004

The *omni-landscape*, outlined in the first chapter, as well as the increasing presence of landscape architecture among the planning disciplines, calls for a debate that, unfortunately, does not really take place. In an age of hybrid concepts (*urban landscape*, landscape urbanism, etc.) and disciplinary metamorphoses, at a historical time in which landscape architecture is in open competition with other construction practices, a critical discussion concerning the possibilities and limits of landscape architecture today appears more than desirable. Such a debate would not only involve landscape architecture, but also architecture, urbanism, land management and, in essence, all the manmade changes imposed to the environment.

On a closer look, however, the level of theoretical reflection in landscape architecture—its methodological self-conscience—remains rather disappointing. Even the label "landscape architecture" is far from being clear. Does the work of a landscape architect today still involve architecture? Does the landscape architect "landscape" (verb), or would it be more correct to talk about interventions on site suitable to be welcomed and interpreted *as* landscape? Do we live in landscapes, as it is often stated, or rather in countries, regions, territories, spaces, that, at a given moment and according to specific conditions, reveal themselves *as* landscapes?

Not raising these questions implies and reinforces the confusion between landscape and territory and contributes to the continuous reification of landscape. Furthermore, it leads to the confusion of the quantitative, measurable and objective aspect with the qualitative and subjective one, typical of the landscape. The map, a simulacrum of the totality as overall view, replaces therefore the somatic perspective experienced on site. Ecological surveys similarly promise to explain the complexity of a given territory, while forgetting the phenomenological complexity. Hence the contemporary trend to identify everything as landscape. Landscape architecture, a dynamic discipline accepted even by its historical antagonists (architects), is the ground on which these problems could and should be dealt with. In order for this to happen, landscape architecture will have to accomplish a triple journey: it has to supply a theory, a hermeneutics and a history of its own know-how..

39 *Industrial waste land*, Lancey, France

The theory of landscape architecture will have to elaborate an intellectual object more complex and exact than the existing ones. Such a theory will allow to deal seriously with the problems of the future, starting from the definition of the discipline (without legislating), analyzing the manifold relations between landscape architecture and other construction practices, including and re-thinking the relationship between landscape and nature, landscape and space, landscape and time, landscape and ecosystems, etc.

The hermeneutical approach concerns not only the methods of 'reading' landscape, but the interpretation of the real life of landscape architecture projects, what John Dixon Hunt calls *afterlife* [24] once the work at the construction site has finished. Hermeneutics implies also a critique of a landscape architecture instead of the usual typological or hagiographic self-presentations. A *history* of landscape architecture—and this may be surprising, after almost two hundred years of practice—is still lacking. The historical sense is underdeveloped within the discipline, both in teaching and in the professional practice. It is not a matter of knowledge in the field of history of art or gardens or other related disciplines; what we really lack is the historical knowledge of the profession and the way it contributed to the transformation of the world. Everything leads to believe that landscape architecture is still afraid of connecting its current practice to what predates it. The discipline evolves—inside frameworks and isolated national traditions—piece by piece, creation after creation, in a disparate and discontinuous way. The lack of theory and of general visibility, the ongoing confusion between landscape and nature, landscape design and environmentalism, landscape and territory, represent the evident external price to pay for this worrisome state of things. The internal price is, if possible, even more onerous: it oonsists in the naïve repetition of automatized actions and the poverty of the formal iatterns rt work in too many contemporary projects. Nhe,great examples of the past and those that come from other cultures—parallel traditions—are, however, not lacking. They should be finally fully acknowledged.

---

[24]. J. Dixon Hunt, *The Afterlife of Gardens,* University of Pennsylvania Press, Philadelphia 2004.

What is Landscape?

Author
Michael Jakob

Editorial Director
Alessandro Franceschini

Published by
LISt Lab
info@listlab.eu
listlab.eu

Art Director
& Graphic Design
Blacklist Creative, BCN
blacklist-creative.com

ISBN 9788898774999

Printed and bound
in European Union,
July 2018

all rights reserved
© of the edition LISt Lab;
© of the text the authors;
© of the images the authors.

series **BABEL**

Prohibited total or partial
reproduction of this book by any means,
without permission of the author
and Publisher.

Promotion and distribution in Italy
Messaggerie Libri, Spa, Milano,
Numero verde 800.804.900
assistenza.ordini@meli.it;

International promotion and distribution
ACC Book Distribution Ltd
Woodbridge, Suffolk, IP12 4SD, UK
sales@antique-acc.com

Sientific Board of LIStLab Editions
Eve Blau (Harvard GSD), Maurizio Carta (Università di Palermo), Alfredo Ramirez (Architectural Association London) Alberto Clementi (Università di Chieti), Alberto Cecchetto (Università di Venezia), Stefano De Martino (Università di Innsbruck), Corrado Diamantini (Università di Trento), Antonio De Rossi (Università di Torino), Franco Farinelli (Università di Bologna), Carlo Gasparrini (Università di Napoli), Manuel Gausa (Università di Genova), Giovanni Maciocco (Università di Sassari/Alghero), Antonio Paris (Università di Roma), Mosè Ricci (Università di Trento), Roger Riewe (Università di Graz), Pino Scaglione (Università di Trento).

LISt Lab is an editorial workshop, based in Europe, that works on contemporary issues. LISt Lab not only publishes, but also researches, proposes, promotes, produces, creates networks.

LISt Lab is a green company committed to respect the environment. Paper, ink, glues and all processings come from short supply chains and aim at limiting pollution. The print run of books and magazines is based on consumption patterns, thus preventing waste of paper and surpluses. LISt Lab aims at the responsibility of the authors and markets, towards the knowledge of a new publishing culture based on resource management.